Books by Ralph Moody
Available in Bison Books editions

The Dry Divide
The Fields of Home
The Home Ranch
Horse of a Different Color
Little Britches
Man of the Family
Mary Emma & Company
Shaking the Nickel Bush
Stagecoach West

Mary Emma
& Company

By RALPH MOODY

Illustrated by Tran Mawicke

University of Nebraska Press
Lincoln and London

First Bison Book printing: 1994

Library of Congress Cataloging-in-Publication Data
Moody, Ralph, 1898–
Mary Emma & company / by Ralph Moody; illustrated by Tran Mawicke.
p.   cm.
ISBN 0-8032-8211-7 (pbk.)
1. Family—Massachusetts—Fiction.   2. Widows—Massachusetts—Fiction.   I. Title.   II. Title: Mary Emma and company.
PS3563.05535M37   1994
813'.54—dc20
93-43936   CIP

Reprinted by arrangement with Edna Moody Morales and Jean S. Moody

∞

TO

MARY EMMA

Contents

1. A Look Around   11
2. Breaking in a Bike   17
3. The Bad-Boy Book   25
4. "A Pleasant Little Walk"   37
5. Molasses on the Loose   44
6. "Pop Goes the Weasel"   52
7. A Pretty Reasonable Fellow   64
8. A Bigger Chunk than We Can Chew   75
9. Not a Bit Professional   83
10. Sunday in Our New Home   94
11. The Furnace Expert   108
12. Full Speed Ahead   119
13. Tricks of the Trade   127
14. What an Ambitious Boy   136
15. A Mite 'o Dickerin'   143
16. Housewarming   152
17. Another Mark Against Me   162

18. DAREDEVIL GRACE   170
19. NEW CUSTOMERS   181
20. NEVER PICK ON AN ALDERMAN'S SON   187
21. FIRE!   195
22. THE LAW OF SALVAGE   206
23. EVERY LITTLE BIT HELPS   217
24. A MAY BASKET FOR MARY EMMA   226

MARY EMMA & COMPANY

1

A Look Around

FATHER died in March, 1910, soon after we'd moved to Littleton, Colorado, from a ranch near the mountains. That was five months before my youngest sister, Elizabeth, was born, but we didn't have too much trouble in making our own living. Mother and my older sister, Grace, did baking that we sold around the village, and laundered lace curtains for one of the big hotels in Denver. The younger children picked fruit and berries, or helped me gather coal along the railroad. And because we kept a horse I could always find jobs when I wasn't in school; hauling discarded railroad ties to cut into kindling and sell, or working on one of the ranches, or riding for the cattle drover in Littleton.

On New Year's Day, 1912, our good friend, Sheriff McGrath, came to our house and talked to Mother for nearly an hour. After he'd gone she called Grace and me in and told us, "Children, I have to make the greatest decision of my life—possibly of our lives—and I need your help. I'm sure you remember Mr. Loediker, the crazy Dutchman who lived on the ranch next to ours. He has been arrested and accused of an old crime for

11

which he was not morally responsible. If Father were still with us I'm sure he would be able to clear Mr. Loediker, but what little I know of the matter would tend to convict him rather than acquit him.

"Sheriff McGrath tells me that I shall doubtlessly be subpoenaed within the next few days to testify in court against Mr. Loediker. But I feel certain that he was also trying to tell me, without exactly saying so, that I am free to come and go as I choose until served with the subpoena. If I were not in Colorado, if I could not be found when the subpoena is issued, the prosecution would have to be dropped for lack of evidence. But if we should leave this state we would have to leave everything we have and love. It would take every penny we have in the bank and nearly everything that could be raised quickly from the sale of our belongings just to buy railroad tickets. Children, I am not sure. I have prayed and prayed, and I have tried to think what Father would say if he were still with us, but my mind is so confused. Ralph, what do you think Father would say?"

I didn't have to think. I said, "I *know* what Father would say, don't you, Grace?"

"Of course I know," Grace said, "and he wouldn't be afraid of what might happen to us." Then she turned to Mother and said, "We're not little children any longer; Ralph's thirteen now, and I'm nearly fifteen. We've been able to make a good living here for nearly two years and I'll bet we can do just as well anywhere else. Do you have any idea where we might go?"

For a minute or two Mother sat looking at her folded hands. Then she looked up quickly and said, "My good brother Frank lives near Boston. He will take us in until we can find a place for ourselves. Boston is a big city, and we should find something there that we can do to make our living."

At a few minutes before midnight on January second we took the train out of Denver, and a few minutes before midnight on January fifth Uncle Frank met us when we got off the train at the North Station in Boston. Within half an hour we were at his house in Medford.

Mother was right when she said her brother Frank would take us in until we could make a place for ourselves, but how in the world he and Aunt Hilda did it I hardly know. They lived in the downstairs half of a double house on Lawrence Street that had one bedroom beside their own. Their baby, Louise, was only two months old, and John was less than two years. It was past midnight and the temperature was down to zero when we got there, but Aunt Hilda had hot chocolate and cake and cookies waiting for us. And if she wasn't as glad to have us come as we were to be there, nobody could ever have guessed it. I liked her from the first minute I saw her. She was tall and pretty, her voice was low in her throat, and she talked with just a tinge of brogue.

I'd seen Uncle Frank before we moved to Colorado in 1906. He'd come to our house the year Father had to be in bed with tuberculosis, but I didn't remember him very well. Coming from Boston to Medford he'd talked to Mother all the way, so I didn't have any chance to get acquainted with him again. But before we'd been in his house fifteen minutes I felt as if I'd known him all my life. He didn't treat me as if I were a little boy, and he had the knack of making people laugh without trying to be funny. As soon as I'd finished my chocolate and cookies he called to me, "Come on there, partner, it's about time we was gettin' this herd bedded down for the night." Mother must have told him I'd worked on the cattle ranches, and he said it just the way any cowhand on the Y-B spread might have said it.

Except for a cook's fire and a chuckwagon, the house did look sort of like a roundup camp when we were finished. Mother and Elizabeth slept in the one spare bedroom, and the rest of us slept on shake-downs on the parlor floor. They looked like cowhands' bedrolls around a campfire.

It wasn't quite daylight next morning when Mother woke me quietly and motioned for me to follow her into her room. Grace was already there, sitting on the edge of the bed with her feet hunkered up under her nightgown. I sat down near her, then

Mother sat between us and whispered, "When we came here I didn't realize that we would be virtually crowding Uncle Frank and Aunt Hilda out of their own home, but that is exactly what we're doing, and we mustn't stay here any longer than is absolutely necessary. I shall get right out early this morning and see what can be found in the way of a place where we can live —and what can be picked up inexpensively in the way of second-hand furniture. Then I shall go in to Boston and inquire about getting curtains to launder for hotels, just as we did for the Brown Palace in Denver."

She put an arm around each of us and went on, "Gracie, I want you to help Aunt Hilda in every way you can, but you must be careful not to be too aggressive. It is a part of your nature that you will have to watch. No woman likes to have another come into her home and try to change her way of doing things. And, Ralph, you might take Muriel and Philip and Hal for a nice long walk this forenoon. That will keep you all out from under Aunt Hilda's feet, and will give you an opportunity to find out where your school is situated. Now run along, both of you, and lie quietly until you hear Uncle Frank and Aunt Hilda getting up. They are probably not used to rising as early as we do, and we must accommodate ourselves to their customs."

I took the children for a walk right after breakfast, but I didn't go looking for any schoolhouses. Ever since Father died Mother had let me stay out of school whenever I could find a job that paid fifty cents a day or more. And I thought that if I hurried up and found myself a good job like that right away, she might not make me go back to school at all. But there was something else that I wanted even more than a good job and not having to go to school. I wanted a job with a horse.

There had hardly been a time since I was eight years old when I didn't have a horse to take care of, and to ride and drive, and I knew that I'd be lonesome without one. But I had sense enough to know that there wouldn't be any cattle to herd around an eastern city, and that jobs with horses would probably be

scarce. I'd thought about it a lot when I'd had nothing else to
do on the train, and there was only one answer I could find:
every city would have to have grocery stores, and grocery stores
had to have delivery wagons, and wherever there was a delivery
wagon there'd have to be at least one horse.

From the second we'd stepped off the train in Medford I'd
kept my eye peeled for a grocery store, and I found one within
two minutes. The Glenwood Station in Medford was half a block
down the railroad tracks from a street that had four or five stores
on it, and the D & H Grocery was right on the corner where
the sidewalk from the depot met the street.

After Mother sent Grace and me back to bed that morning, I
had to lie quiet for a long time before I heard Uncle Frank getting up, but it gave me a good chance to do a little planning. I
knew I couldn't get out of taking the children for a walk, but I
wasn't going to let that get in the way of my trying to get a job
in the D & H Grocery just as fast as I could. For a little while I
was worried about going in to ask for a job while I had three
little children with me. It didn't seem quite businesslike. Then
I got an idea that made it seem better that way than any other.

Whenever I'd earned any money I'd always taken it all home
to Mother, but she knew I sort of liked to have a little change in
my pocket, so she'd always give me back a dime or a nickel that
I could keep for myself. That morning I knew that I had seventeen cents: a dime, a nickel, and two pennies. I wasn't sure when
I'd be able to earn any more, so I kind of wanted to hold onto it
all, but I thought the time had come when it would be best to
spend some. I could hardly walk into the D & H Grocery with
three little children and tell the owner that I'd come looking for
a job driving his delivery wagon. But if we just went in as if I'd
come to buy them some candy there'd be a good excuse for their
being there, and I'd have a little better chance to talk to the man
if we'd come in as customers. For a while I thought about spending the odd two cents, but I remembered Mother's saying once
that it didn't pay to be too pinch-penny, so I decided that I'd
spend the whole nickel.

Spring Street ran a little downhill at the railroad crossing, and the door of the D & H Grocery was at the foot of the hill, so that one end of it was almost in a cellar, and the plate glass window at the upper end was only about two feet high. That made it sort of hard to see into, but I wanted to look the store over in good shape, and pick out which one of the men would be the boss, before I went in to spend my nickel and ask him for a job.

The first time we walked by I couldn't see anybody in the store; just a calico cat, curled up and asleep on the counter. Then, when we came back past on the other side of the street, there was a short, fat man behind the counter, leaning on it and stroking the cat. The candy case was right beside him, straight in from the door. That time I walked the children a couple of blocks down Spring Street before we came back, so that if the man had seen us go by twice he wouldn't think I was spying. When we came back the cat was off the counter and there was a second man behind it, grinding coffee. He wasn't much taller than the fat man, but thin, and quick in his movements.

From the way he was working I was pretty sure the thin man would be the boss, and I wanted to wait until he was through grinding coffee before we went in, so I stalled for a few minutes, letting Hal try to count the oranges in one of the windows. As soon as the man was through grinding the coffee he put it in a bag, tied it, and went quickly to weigh some crackers that he took out of a tin box. I could see that there wasn't much chance of getting him to wait on us, so I took Hal by the hand and we all went in.

2

Breaking in a Bike

ALL the way up and down Spring Street, and even before I got up that morning, I'd been planning and rehearsing just what I'd say when I asked for the job, but the minute we were inside the store I forgot every word of it. I tried to remember some of it as the children looked into the candy case, making up their minds what they wanted, but the fat man didn't give me much chance to think. As soon as he'd said, "Good morning," he asked, "Newcomers in the neighborhood?"

"Yes, sir," I told him. "We just got here last night."

"Well, well, well, is that so?" he said, with sort of a little chuckle. "Where from? The West? You don't talk like you come from raight around these parts."

I'd noticed that he—and even Uncle Frank—talked a bit different from the people in Colorado, a little bit flatter or something; but I didn't know how the man could tell we'd come from the West, so I just said, "Yes, sir. Colorado."

"Where you livin'?" he asked.

"Well, right now we're staying with my Uncle Frank—Mr. Gould, on Lawrence Street," I told him, "but Mother has gone to see if she can find us a house of our own."

"Well now, that's good. Hope she finds one close by. What does your pa do?" he asked.

"He died nearly two years ago," I told him. Then I thought that might be about as good a time as any to ask him about a job, so I said, "That's why I'm looking for a job. I've worked on ranches for the past four summers, and we've always had at least one horse of our own, and I know how to take good care of them, and to mend harness, and to keep wagon wheels greased, and I could do a real good job of driving your delivery wagon, and I'd work for fifty cents a day, and I don't care how long the hours are."

"Well, well, well," he said, and chuckled some more, "that's pretty good for a little shaver like you, but. . . ."

I thought I'd better head him off before he had a chance to say I was too small for the job, so I broke right in. "I know I'm not very big, but I'm a lot stronger than I look, and I can handle a full-grown steer at the end of a rope. Last summer I worked a hundred straight days on Batchlet's Home Ranch, and he paid me a dollar a day—full cowhand wages."

"*My, my, my!*" he said that time, and his chuckle came awfully close to being a laugh. "You look a mite small for a cowhand. Come 'round here to the scales, and let's see how much you weigh."

I knew how much I weighed: seventy-two pounds. I'd weighed the same for three years, but I'd grown nearly three inches and was a lot stronger than when I was nine. I got my mouth open to tell the man, and then I thought better of it. It seemed to me that if I went around there behind the counter and let him weigh me I'd be at least part way in, and that I'd have a better chance of getting the job.

After I'd told the children they could pick out anything they wanted, up to five cents' worth, I went around and stood on the big scale beside the potato bin. The man tapped the weight along with one finger until the beam balanced, then dropped his glasses down off his forehead, peered at the beam, and said, "Seventy-two pounds, raight on the mark. How old be you?"

"Thirteen," I told him, "three weeks ago, but I'm strong for my age." There was a bushel basket, nearly full of potatoes, sitting in front of the bin, so I lifted it knee-high to show him.

"Well, well, well," he said again, "you are pretty stout for a little shaver, but I couldn't hire you to drive our delivery wagon, 'cause we ain't got one. Can you ride a bicycle?"

"I don't know," I said. "I never tried to ride one, but I guess I could. I've ridden some pretty mean horses."

That time he laughed right out loud. "A bicycle can be a mean critter, too, when you're first learnin' to ride it," he told me. "How much did you say you wanted?"

"Fifty cents a day, and I don't care how long the hours are," I said.

"Well, well! Now don't you think that's a little steep for a boy before and after school?"

"Mother doesn't make me go to school when I can find a job that pays fifty cents a day or more," I told him.

"Hmmm, hmmmm, well," he said, "your ma wouldn't have much to say about that here in Mass'chusetts: they'd have the truant officer after you."

I didn't know what a truant officer was, but I could see there wouldn't be much chance of my staying out of school, so I said, "Well, I could come as early as you wanted me to in the mornings before school, and stay as late as the store is open after school, and work all day on Saturdays, and I could do that for half price."

"Dollar and a half a week?" he asked.

Of course I knew that, at a dollar and a half a week, I'd be throwing in a full day's work on Saturday at the same price as a school day, but I wanted the job—even if they didn't have a horse—so I said, "Yes, sir, I'd make a deal that way if I could count on having fifty cents a day when school vacation time comes."

Instead of answering me the fat man called to the other one, "John, there's a boy here wants to hire out to us for a dollar and a half a week. He's a little shaver, but stout for his size, and from the way he goes about makin' a dicker I calc'late he'd turn out to be a good merchant. What you think?"

The other man stopped his work just long enough to look at me for half a minute over the top of his glasses, then called back, "He appears awful small for a delivery boy, but use your own judgment, Gus."

I was too close to let the chance get by, so before the man named Gus could say anything, I made my best offer. "I'll work a week for nothing," I told him. "That way, it won't cost you anything to find out that I can handle the job."

I think that's what got me the job, and I'm sure it was what got the children a whole bag of candy for nothing. He picked a piece out of every tray in the case, then passed the bag to me and said, "That's to bind the bargain; you be here at seven o'clock tomorrow mornin' to sweep up and bag some coal." Then, as we were going out, he called me back and said, "If you want, you could come 'round about six o'clock this evenin' and get the bicycle, so's to get in a little practice on it."

I was so happy about getting a job my first day in town that I wanted to dance, but I wouldn't let myself, because I didn't really have it for sure; just sort of on a week's trial. I got thinking about that as soon as we were outside the store, and it seemed to me that the best thing I could do to get ready for my new job was to learn the street names, so I walked the children all around that end of Medford till noon.

In the afternoon the children were too tired to go out at all, but Grace made me go and find out which school we'd go to and what the teachers' names would be. I found that Philip and Muriel would go to the James School, and that I'd go to the Franklin. Hal wasn't old enough to go, and Grace wasn't going. She'd been in the eighth grade when Father died, but after that she had to stay at home to help Mother.

That afternoon seemed ten times as long to me as the forenoon had, mostly because I didn't have much of anything to do, and because I was anxious for six o'clock to come, so I could find out whether or not I could ride the grocery store bicycle. I'd seen plenty of people ride bicycles—some of them girls, and some of them sitting up straight and riding no-hands—so I knew it couldn't be very hard, but I wanted to be real sure I could do it before I started my new job.

Partly because I was worried about Mother, and partly because I wanted to have another look at the bicycle down at the grocery store, I went to meet every train that came in after four o'clock. It was half-past-five before Mother came, and when she stepped down from the car she looked tired and worried. I ran right to her, took the bundle she was carrying, and told her about my new job. I didn't tell her that it was only for a week's trial, or that I'd said I'd work that week for nothing.

She laid her hand on my shoulder and said, "You've done a great deal better than your mother has, Son. From what I've been able to learn, most of the larger hotels in Boston launder and stretch their own lace curtains, and the others pay so small a price that we couldn't make a living by doing their work. On the other hand, rents are terribly high here, and I didn't see a stick of used furniture that was worth anything like the price they were asking for it. I shall look again tomorrow, but it may be that we will find Medford is not the right place for us." For a minute or two she walked along with her lips pinched tight, then she said sternly, as if she had forgotten I was there, "We shall not impose on Frank and Hilda; they have all they can do to take care of their own little ones."

I don't know what more she might have said if Uncle Frank hadn't called, "Hi, Mary Emma!" from in back of us. Until Mother turned I didn't know it was Uncle Frank calling, or that the call was for her. Father had always called her "Mame," so had all her best friends in Colorado, and I wasn't used to hearing her called "Mary Emma."

Uncle Frank had been on the same train Mother came on, but had ridden back in the smoker, so she hadn't seen him. I ran back to meet him, and told him about my new job and the bicycle, but when we caught up to Mother they talked about lace curtains. She didn't say a word about the high prices of rents, or that Medford might not be the right place for us.

Aunt Hilda and Grace had supper ready when we reached the house, but it was so near six o'clock that I didn't dare stop to eat. I carried the bundle inside, then ran right back for the bicycle. I didn't try to get on it, but pushed it, and that was hard enough. It must have weighed just about as much as I did, there was a big basket strapped to the handle bars, the tires were made of solid rubber, and the snow hadn't been shoveled off more than half of the sidewalks.

Uncle Frank said he'd help me with learning to ride the bicycle, but not until after I'd eaten my supper, so I poked down the plateful Aunt Hilda had saved for me just as fast as I could. Then Uncle Frank helped me shovel off two of the neighbors' walks, so that I'd have a good clear stretch of sidewalk to ride on.

As soon as the walks were cleared he stood the bike at one end of the runway we'd made, and said, "Now I'll ride it a little piece to show you how. There's only one trick to it: when you feel it beginning to tip toward either side, turn the handle bars that way and you'll straighten it right up. Now you watch how I do it."

As he was talking he lifted the hind wheel off the sidewalk, reached down, and turned the foot pedal on his side around until it was straight up. Then, after he'd told me to watch him, he stepped up on it, threw the other leg over—just as if he'd been mounting a horse—and away he went. I couldn't see that he turned the handle bars at all, but he went right down the middle of the sidewalk, turned the bicycle around, and pedaled it as straight back to me as if he'd been riding on a tightrope.

Before I tried to get on I was careful to lift the hind wheel and turn the pedal around just as he had, but when I stepped up onto it the bike came over onto me quicker than a horse that's stepped into a gopher hole. It was lucky that there was a good high snow bank along there, so I didn't get hurt a bit. When I'd picked myself up and got the snow out of my ears,

Uncle Frank said, "Don't pull the handle bars toward you when you go up; leave them straight. It's time enough to turn them when you get rolling."

I tried it the same way three more times, but each time the bike pitched me into the snow bank before we'd gone a foot. I found out what the trouble was on that third fall. "I know what I'm doing wrong," I told Uncle Frank. "With a strange horse you always pull his head way around toward you before you go up. That way he can't rear, or start off too quick and dump you. Next time I'll remember not to pull the handle bars around as I'm going up."

I didn't pull them, but I must have pushed. Anyway, the bike ran into the snow bank on the other side of the walk, and I dived head-first into a low hedge with a million little thorns on it. I didn't get scratched up very much, but I was pretty sore at myself for not being able to do something that lots of girls could do. Uncle Frank helped me get untangled from the hedge, and asked, "Are you hurt?"

I wasn't, but I wouldn't have let on if I had been. "No, sir," I told him, "but I wish there was some way to put a gunny sack over this critter's eyes, the way they put one over a horse's eyes in a roundup. Then they can't buck till you're all on and have both feet in the stirrups."

He told me he'd be the gunny sack, so he stood in front of the bike on my next try, holding the handle bars with his hands and the wheel between his knees. Everything went fine until he stepped away, and for about six feet after that, then the bike decided to go one way just as I decided to go the other, and I was in the hedge again.

On my fourth try after that I made as much as twenty feet before it pitched me off again, going down the sidewalk as if both the bicycle and I were drunk.

"That's fine! That's fine!" Uncle Frank told me as he came to help me out of the hedge. "Your only trouble is that you don't turn the handle bars quick enough when you begin to tip, and then, when you do turn them, you turn too far."

"I know it," I told him, "but I don't know what to do about it. I can always tell which way a bucking horse is going to jump by the way he turns his ears, but this thing doesn't give you any warning."

I was scratched up from the hedge more than I thought, but I guess I looked a lot worse off than I really was. When I wiped my mitten across my face it came away with a red smooch on it, and Uncle Frank said, "That's enough for one lesson. Those solid tires and the basket will always make it tough to ride, but after another day or two you won't have to think anything about keeping it balanced. I'll drop in at the store in the morning and tell Gus Haushalter that you're going to make out all right, but that you'd better deliver your orders on Shank's mare for the rest of this week."

There were plenty of days on the ranches when I worked a lot harder than I had that day, but I don't remember ever being any more tired. That evening Uncle Frank tried to teach me how to play cribbage, but I went to sleep right in the middle of a game.

3

The Bad-Boy Book

I DON'T know how early it was when I first woke up the next morning—or even if it was morning—but I must have dozed off just a few seconds before Uncle Frank shook me and whispered, "Time to get up, fella. It's quarter after six, and I've got a bite to eat ready in the kitchen."

Whewwww, it was cold that first morning when I started for work at the D & H Grocery, and the bicycle pushed as if it weighed half a ton. The cold was a different kind from what we had in Colorado. It made tears come into my eyes, and a drop on the end of my nose, but I needed both hands to keep the bike from tipping over, so I couldn't do anything about it.

The yellow light from the big kerosene lamp above the counter was shining out onto the snow as I came down the hill past the store windows, and Mr. Haushalter was building a fire in the pot-bellied stove that stood in the middle of the floor. It wasn't nearly as cold inside the store as it was outside, but he still had on his overcoat, and a red woolen muffler wound around his neck. He looked up as I opened the door, and said, "Well, well, well, right on time! That's the ticket! Nippy out this mornin', ain't it?"

"Yes, sir," I said. "Shall I bring the bicycle inside?"

"No need, no need," he told me. "John'll be along after a while, and he'll want it for goin' to get his orders. Hold on a minute whilst I go fetch some kerosene. Didn't bank this cussed fire high enough last night and it petered out on me."

He didn't seem to be in any hurry, and sort of waddled—like a fat duck—as he went behind the counter and through a doorway into a back room. He was gone three or four minutes, then waddled back, holding an old quart measure in his hand. He opened the stove door, tossed in about a cupful of kerosene, and jumped back. It was a good thing that he jumped quick. In less than a tenth of a second the stove belched out a peck of ashes and a bushel of flame. The lid on top of it jumped three or four inches into the air, and a cloud of black smoke went up to the ceiling. "There," Mr. Haushalter said as he kicked the stove door shut, "that ought to do the trick. Come get your hands warm, and I'll show you abouts; then you can sweep out some. Ain't had a boy for two-three months now, and the place is gettin' a mite dusty. Kitty-kitty-kitty."

I was sure Mr. Haushalter had lit the stove that same way a good many times. The ceiling above it was as black as a coal bin, there was a gray layer of dust and ashes on the shelves nearby, and I'd noticed that the calico cat sneaked away under the cracker case when she saw him coming with the quart measure. As he talked to me he went back to the counter, reached under, and set up a two-gallon milk can.

"Nights in this kind of weather there ain't no sense puttin' it in the ice box; keeps sweet enough right under the counter," he told me as he stooped down and brought up a chipped cereal bowl: the kind with red flowers on it that always came in Banner Oats. "Kitty-kitty-kitty," he called again as he filled the bowl and set it on the floor. Then, as the cat crawled out from under the cracker case, he looked up at me and said, "Whenst you go to cleanin' up, don't sweep too close to the cracker case. Matilda's got a new litter of kittens under there—fourth litter she's had since spring if I recollect rightly. You can come along now

if you're thawed out a mite; I'll show you abouts. Let me see, you said you was Frank Gould's nephew, but I don't recollect you sayin' what your first name is."

"It's Ralph," I said, "Ralph Moody."

"Oh, then your ma is Frank's sister . . . or be you kin to his wife?"

"Mother's Mr. Gould's sister," I said as I went behind the counter with him, but he didn't seem to be listening. "Hmmmmm, Moody," he said. "Hope you ain't *too* moody. John, he gets that way sometimes when business is off a dite, but I can't see much sense to it. Business comes and business goes, kind of like the tide. Can't expect it to be at flood all the time. Got a middle name?"

"Yes, sir," I said. "It's Owen."

Mr. Haushalter stopped right where he was, and chuckled so hard that the ends of his muffler jiggled. "Owen . . . Owen," he said, and then chuckled again. "Owen Moore, he went away, owin' more than he could pay. Owen Moore come back again, owin' more." He didn't say it as if he were saying it to me, or as if he were making fun of my name. It was more as if he'd just thought of something he hadn't heard for a long, long time, and was saying it over to himself.

"Well, well, well," he said as he started on again, "owin' is bad business." He stopped again, right behind the candy case, looked at me sternly, and said, "So's stealin', and I don't want you to ever steal as much as one pea bean around here."

I couldn't have felt much worse if he'd slapped me, but before I could think of a word to say he chuckled again and went on, "So there's the candy case, and yonder is the cookie case, and the cheese box, and there's apples in the barrel. A boy's got to eat, and there's nothin' will make a thief out of him any quicker'n an empty belly, so eat all you want. You'll prob'ly get sick on candy the first couple of days—most boys does—but you'll simmer down 'fore the week's out. Now there's just one more thing I want to tell you: that's only for yourself, and only right here in the store; you don't take stuff out with you, and you don't give it to nobody else—not even your own brothers and sisters. Is that fair?"

"Yes, sir," I told him. "That's more than fair. And that way I could afford to work for . . ."

"Never mind the 'sir,' " he broke in. "Everybody calls me Gus, and they call John, John. But if you've a mind to, you could call John, Mr. Durant; I have a notion he'd like it. Well, well, we've frittered away a lot of time here, ain't we? And here comes John now. You might as well get on with the sweepin'— and take care 'bout the kittens. Broom's in the corner, yonder by the coal scuttle. I'll show you 'round some more after school's over; you're commencin' today, ain't you?"

Mother had already taken Muriel and Philip over to the James School, and was waiting for me when I'd finished the sweeping and got back to Uncle Frank's house at quarter of nine. But I didn't like the cap she was holding in her hand a single bit. Two summers before, the cowhands on the Y-B Ranch had given me a genuine Stetson hat—not a ten-gallon, but a five. That kind of a hat will last for years and years if you take good care of it, and they'd bought one that was about a size too big, so it would still fit me after I'd grown some more. The only trouble was that I'd just about stopped growing, but the hat fit all right if I kept some folded paper inside the sweat band. I'd never had anything to wear that I liked as much as I liked that hat, and I'd taken real fine care of it, so that it was almost as good as new. But Mother didn't think it was the right kind of a hat for me to wear to school in Medford, and had bought me a stocking cap when she'd been in Boston the day before. She put it on me and pulled it down over my ears as soon as I came in. To make it worse, it was a girl's cap instead of a boy's; white, with a fluffy red ball on the top.

Of course, I didn't tell Mother I wouldn't wear the cap, but I came as close to it as I dared. I did tell her that the boys would think I was a sissy if I wore it, and that if a fellow got the name of sissy tacked onto him his first day in a new school he could almost never get over it. That's what made her let me wear my Stetson, but it didn't keep me out of trouble.

Just because I'd happened to get into a scrap or two, Mother always worried whenever I went into a new school. I know she was worried that day. As we walked down Spring Street and over Central Avenue toward the Franklin School, she told me, "It is against my better judgment to let you wear this hat the cowboys gave you. In Colorado it was quite all right, but here it will look simply ridiculous. I am letting you wear it this one day only, and for one reason only: so that you may not feel obliged to pick a fight in order to prove your manliness. I will not *tolerate* your fighting in this new school. Now what did you tell me the principal's name was?"

"Well, I think Mr. Haushalter said it was Jackman, but it might have been Jackson. I tried to remember it but . . ."

"Never mind!" Mother told me sharply. "Whatever it is, I shall tell him to let me know immediately if you give him the slightest particle of trouble. And I want you to keep your wits about you while we are talking to him. I believe your number-work, reading and geography are good enough so that you might go into the eighth grade instead of the seventh."

Mother could almost always make friends with people the first time she met them, but she didn't make friends with Mr. Jackman that first day I went to school in Medford, and I didn't either. As soon as they'd told each other their names and she'd told him mine, she said, "Ralph has been in the seventh grade in Colorado, but his teacher thought he was nearly ready for eighth-grade work; his arithmetic, reading and geography are really quite good."

Mr. Jackman was a big man; fat, with a shiny bald head and pink cheeks. He didn't look quite as old as Mother, but he was more than a foot taller, and he left us standing, so that she had to turn her face up when she talked to him. Before she had finished he was looking down at her with the same kind of a smile that Grace used to give me when she was going to call me a ninny. "Most mothers think their children are brighter than the average," he said, "but you must remember, Mrs. Moody, that our schools here in Massachusetts are quite advanced as compared to a state such as Colorado."

From the way Mother's face turned pale I knew she was provoked, but she smiled right back and said, "I am well aware of a mother's weaknesses, but I believe that if you give Ralph an examination you will find . . ."

Mr. Jackman didn't let her finish, but looked down at me and asked, "What is the result of twelve times twelve, divided by thirteen, times five, divided by three?"

I got along all right until I came to fifty-five and five-thirteenths, then I got a little bit mixed up in trying to divide it by three, and Mr. Jackman mixed me up more by saying, "Come, come, boy! What is the answer?"

"I don't know," I told him. "I got mixed up when I got into the thirteenths. In Colorado we only had . . ."

He didn't let me tell him that we had only up to twelfths, but shook his head and said, "Hmmph! Well, where is Narragansett Bay?"

I'd never even heard of Narragansett Bay, but I didn't want to seem stupid, and it did have sort of a French sound to it, so I just made a guess and said, "On the coast of France."

That time Mr. Jackman laughed right out loud, shook his head again, and told Mother, "We'll try him in the seventh grade, but I have my doubts."

By that time Mother's face was plain white and she had her lips pinched together. "Very well," she said, and started to leave the office. At the door she turned back and said, "Mr. Jackman, I shall expect you to let me know if you have the slightest trouble with Ralph—either in his studies or otherwise." Then she walked out without saying another word.

I didn't have a bit of trouble in class; my teacher was a good one, the reading was easy, and the arithmetic problems were in quarters and eighths instead of thirteenths. But at recess time I didn't get along very well. It all started over my hat. We hadn't been out in the yard two minutes before some one of the boys knocked it off. Then, as fast as I could pick it up, brush it off, and put it on again, some other boy knocked it off. In Colorado I'd have tried to lick the first boy who did it, but in Medford there were two reasons why I didn't dare. Mother always meant it when she said she wouldn't tolerate anything, and besides, Mr. Jackman was out there in the school yard with us. I knew he couldn't have helped seeing what was going on, and I was sure he'd stop the boys as soon as he saw that I wasn't going to fight—but he didn't.

About the tenth time my hat got knocked off the folded paper I kept inside the sweat band came out. Of course, that made it a size too big for my head, and the next boy jerked it down over my face so hard I was afraid he'd tear the brim. Before I straightened it out and put it back on I looked all around and said, "The next one that touches my hat is going to get poked in the nose."

Al Richardson was the one who did it, and so quick that I didn't have a chance to get my fists doubled up before the hat brim was jerked clear down to my chin. To make it worse, the sweat band caught on my nose when I tried to pull the hat up, and I had to stand there like a cat trying to get its head out of a salmon can while all the boys laughed at me. That would have made me mad enough but, on top of it, I could hear Mr. Jackman laughing, too. His voice was high, like a woman's, and his laugh was almost a squeal.

I don't know whether I made my nose bleed when I finally managed to yank the hat off, or whether Al did it. It could have been either one, because there was only a second from the time I got my hat off until we were fighting. I could punch twice as hard as Al, but he could hit twice as fast, and he could duck quicker than the bobber on a trout line. That was what got me into my first big trouble in Medford: Al ducked, but Mr. Jackman didn't.

He must have come to pull us apart just as I started a hay-maker, and he must have been bending over, because my left fist caught him square in the right eye. For what seemed to me like ten minutes he just stood there rubbing his eye, as if he couldn't believe what had happened to him. I told him that I didn't mean to do it and was sorry, but he grabbed me by the

shoulders of my coat and shook me until I thought my teeth would rattle loose. After he'd stopped he told me, between pantings, to march right back to my room, and that I'd have no more recesses until I'd learned to be civilized.

I felt real bad about it until recess was over and Al Richardson came back to class. He sat right across the aisle from me, and he had a good big lump on his cheekbone, but he wasn't sore about it. As soon as Miss Bradley turned her back to draw a map on the blackboard, he leaned over and whispered, "You can sock pretty hard, but I'll bet I can lick you. After school, if we get a chance?"

I didn't want to get caught whispering on top of everything else, so I just nodded, but we didn't have any fight after school. Al Richardson and Allie Dion walked all the way to the D & H Grocery with me, and all they wanted to do was to have me tell them about Colorado and cowboys and ranches and riding in roundups, and things like that.

That afternoon I was so busy at the grocery store that I forgot all about having had a fight at school, and I only had spare time enough to eat two pieces of candy and a cookie. Quite a few of the families that lived over near the brickyards and the clay pits were poor, and they bought their coal from grocery stores in twenty-five-pound sacks. With the weather having turned cold there were lots of orders, and they kept me going right up to seven o'clock; filling sacks, weighing them, and delivering them on a pushcart.

Supper was over before I'd finished my job and reached Uncle Frank's house, but Aunt Hilda had saved me a big plateful in the kitchen. I was only halfway through it when the doorbell rang. From the kitchen I could hear only a mumble of voices when Uncle Frank went to the door and showed somebody into the parlor. But what I heard next made me lose my appetite and almost wish I'd never had a Stetson hat. A deep voice asked, "Is this Mrs. Moody what has a boy named Ralph in Franklin School?"

Instead of answering, Mother asked in a real worried voice, "What has he done, Officer?"

"Well now," the deep voice went on, " 'twas not till I was after finishin' my beat that I picked up the report at the station house, so I've had no chance to investigate, but if the complaint to the department is true, 'tis very serious."

"Has he been fighting at school?" Mother asked.

"Worse than that," the deep voice boomed, "or I'd not be comin' next nor near to disturb you at this time o' the night. Boys will be boys, and they'll have a tussle now and again, but 'tis the first time in all my forty years on the force that we've had a complaint of a boy attackin' a teacher—leave alone givin' the principal a black eye. If the lad's about, I'd be havin' a word or two to say to him; we'll put up with no bullies here—neither in the schools nor out."

When I was only nine years old Father had taught me that it was always best to go and meet trouble halfway, so I went into the parlor, and I knew the policeman right away. He was Cop Watson. That afternoon he'd come into the store to buy a plug of chewing tobacco. He knew me, too. He'd just finished speaking to Mother when I came into the parlor, but he turned to me and said, "Hello there, bub. Your brother to home?"

"Yes, sir," I told him, "but he's gone to bed. It was me that hit Mr. Jackman."

"You?" he said, with a funny little quirk to his voice. "Was you standin' on a table?"

"No, sir," I told him, "I was standing on my feet. Al Richardson just happened to duck at the wrong time and I hit Mr. Jackman instead. He must have been bent over. I didn't mean to hit him, and I told him so, but I guess he didn't believe me."

Cop Watson had a long white mustache, and when I'd finished he stood smoothing both sides of it with his fingers, as if he were thinking, but Mother said quickly, "Then you *did* get yourself into a fight on your very first day in this new school!"

"Yes, ma'am," I said, "but I couldn't help it. The boys were yanking my hat down over my face and Mr. Jackman was standing right there and he didn't stop them and I had. . . ."

Cop Watson wasn't paying a mite of attention to either Mother or me. I don't think he even heard us, because he broke in and asked, "This Richardson lad. Is he the one lives over on Myrtle Street?"

"I guess so," I told him. "He walked as far as the store with me after school, and then he went up that way."

"And you didn't fight again?"

"No, sir."

Cop Watson smoothed his mustache a stroke or two, then said

to Mother and Uncle Frank, "I'll go have a word with the Richardson lad. I know him; he's a good lad. If there's call for any more investigation I'll be back before bedtime."

When he was almost to the door, he turned, shook a finger at me, and said, "This you'll be havin' to remember: guilty or no, your name's a'ready wrote down on the bad-boy book at the station house and you'll have to be watchin' your step. They keep a sharp eye on the lads what's got their name on the book."

Mother hadn't spanked me since Father died, but I think she would have that night if Uncle Frank hadn't helped me out.

4

"A Pleasant Little Walk"

AFTER that one bad day at school, the rest of our first week in Medford went fine for me. Mr. Haushalter let me wait on some customers, and when Saturday night came he gave me a dollar and a half. He said I had earned every penny of it, and that the job would be mine as long as I tended to business the way I had been doing. Then, besides teaching me how to keep from falling off the bicycle, Uncle Frank taught me to play cribbage. Two nights running, Mother let me sit up till nearly ten o'clock to play with him, and I even beat him once.

Of course, Grace got along all right; she always did. Before the week was out she'd found enough odd jobs, washing dishes and tending babies, that she'd made as much as I did. But Mother didn't have any luck at all. Every day she went to Boston to see if she could find curtains to be laundered and stretched, or furniture that we could afford to buy, but she didn't find either. And I think she looked at every vacant house in the Glenwood end of Medford without finding one that wasn't too much run-down to live in or where the rent wasn't too high. When I got home from work that Saturday night Mother looked as near discouraged as I'd ever seen her, but Sunday seemed to straighten things out for her. After she'd scrubbed my neck until it felt as if she were using sandpaper, she sent the older four of us to Sunday School. Then, when it was time for church service, she came with Hal and Elizabeth. We waited for them at the door, and though Mother never liked to do it, we had to go way up to the front of the church. The third pew was the only one where there was enough room for all of us to sit together.

Grace and I had always liked Sunday School. Maybe it was because we knew more of the Bible stories than the others and could answer more of the lesson questions. But neither of us liked church very well, and I think it was for about the same reason: ever since I could remember—except when we had company or when she was so tired she couldn't keep awake—Mother had read a few verses from the Bible to us before we went to bed. When she read, whether it was the Bible or any other book, it never sounded like reading. She'd glance down at the page for a second or two, then look up at us and tell the story as if she were just talking naturally. None of the ministers we'd ever had did it that way. Some of them sounded as if they were reciting a piece in a Sunday School play, some of them tried to make it sound too grand, and others just read along in a singsong. Most of them preached their sermons the same way they read the scripture.

Mr. Vander Mark, the minister in our new church, read almost exactly the way Mother did, and he didn't read a whole long chapter—only a few verses, and ones that I think I'd always known by heart. Usually, when the minister was reading scripture that I knew, I just sat with my hands folded in my lap and thought about something else until he had finished, but that morning I found myself listening as if it had been a brand-new story.

I don't think Mr. Vander Mark was much older than Mother, and only a couple of inches taller, but he had gray hair and a voice that seemed too big to come from so short a man. It was neither loud nor rough, but filled the whole church—like the low notes from the organ. The big Bible was open on the stand in front of him, but he didn't look down at it. He just folded his arms on it, leaned a bit forward, and talked to us as if Mother and we children were the only ones in the church. If he had known all about us, and that we were going to be there that Sunday, he couldn't have picked any better verses from the whole book: "Ask and it shall be given you; seek and ye shall find; knock, and it shall be opened unto you."

I wish I could remember all that he said after he had finished the reading. I listened to every word of it, but I remember only the meaning instead of the words. He told us that he thought the first verse he had read might be the most misunderstood of all Jesus' teachings, for there was no answer to prayers that were offered in selfishness, or to prayers mumbled into empty space with no real, honest belief that they would be heard and considered by our Heavenly Father. And he told us that ours was a demanding God who expected a full return for every blessing that he gave; that it was a waste of time to pray for help and then sit back with folded hands to wait for it, for help was given only to those who did their very best to help them-selves, but that it was never refused to the deserving.

After the sermon was over Mother put Elizabeth into Grace's arms, and whispered to us, "You children might walk back toward Uncle Frank's house very slowly, and I'll catch up to you. I must stop to say a few words to this minister. I want to tell him how much comfort I have found in his sermon."

Mother must have said a lot more than a few words to Mr. Vander Mark, and he to her. We dawdled all the way back to Uncle Frank's, but she didn't get there for half an hour after we did. But when she came in Grace and I could both see that she wasn't worrying any more. She seemed as happy as she used to when we'd had a real good week in Colorado, and she hummed all the time she was helping Aunt Hilda get dinner ready. Then, when we were at the table, she asked, "Frank, is there a good hand laundry in Medford? When I first worked away from home as a girl I learned to do up all the nice frilly things the ladies used to wear in those days, but I'm afraid I've rather lost the knack of it. I'm sure I could pick it right up again if I could find work in a good hand laundry that specialized in that sort of thing."

Uncle Frank chuckled and said, "Well, there's Sam Lee, down next to Uebel's drug store. If you could learn to write Chinese and iron collars so they felt like files you might get a job with him."

"No, seriously," Mother said.

Then Aunt Hilda told her, "There's one in Malden, Mary Emma, and they do real nice work. I had them do up two shirt-waists for me the last time I went home to Prince Edward Island."

"How far is Malden from here?" Mother asked.

"About half a mile," Uncle Frank told her, "but it's a good big mile to the laundry, and through the roughest part of Edge-worth. I don't think you should try it. It would be mighty hard work and mighty small pay. You'd do better to find something in Boston; housekeeping in a hotel, or something like that, where you'd be bossing others instead of doing the hard work yourself."

"Mmmmm, hmmm, I'll think about it, Frank," Mother said, "but I couldn't do anything that would keep me away from the children very long."

"You'd work from eight in the morning till six at night in a laundry," he told her, "and you wouldn't begin to make a decent living for them; about six dollars a week. Don't be in too big a hurry about finding something to do. We might be a little cramped here, but we'll make out fine until the right thing comes along for you."

"I know, I know, Frank," Mother told him. "You and Hilda would run yourselves into the poorhouse for us if we'd let you, but we must stand on our own feet just as quickly as we can." Then she turned to us and said, "Now clean your plates right up, children. We're going for a nice long walk just as soon as the dishes are done, so that Uncle Frank and Aunt Hilda can have a little rest from our being right under their feet."

As soon as we were out of sight from Uncle Frank's house, Mother had me ask some boys the way to Malden. They told me which would be the shortest way but it was exactly opposite to the way we should have gone. Mother never mentioned the laundry until we were at the far north end of Malden. Then she said, "Now this has been a pleasant little walk, hasn't it? And I didn't notice anything rough about any of the neighborhoods we came through. Ralph, suppose you ask some of those young men over there at the corner where we might find the hand laundry. Since we are so near we may as well drop by and look at it. I shall want to know right where to find it in the morning."

While I was gone to ask for directions Grace must have been telling Mother the same things that Uncle Frank had told her at the dinner table. I got back just in time to hear Mother saying, "No, dear, I shall have to use my own best judgment in this matter. I have no intention of spending the rest of my life working in a laundry, but I must do it long enough to learn all I can about the professional manner of starching, ironing, and packing fine laundry. Ralph, did you find out the best way for us to go?"

"Yes, ma'am," I told her, "on the streetcar. We've come the wrong way and it's nearly two miles from here to the laundry."

"Hmmmm, well," Mother said, "and it would cost us twenty cents each way. I think maybe we'd better walk. If we don't try to hurry, and take turns in carrying Elizabeth, two miles won't seem very far. The exercise and fresh air might do us all good."

As soon as we'd started along again she went right on talking to Grace, just as though she'd never interrupted herself. "Until you are all grown and ready to have homes of your own, I will *not* be separated from you children for a moment longer than is absolutely necessary. That means that we must find some way of making our living in our own home. There is sewing, knitting, and embroidery that one may take home to do for factories, but if we were all to work at it as hard as we could go, we would make only a bare existence. On the other hand, I find that there are a good many well-to-do families in Medford; people who have expensive garments and who are glad to pay a generous price to have them beautifully laundered. I shall work in the best hand laundry I can find, at whatever wages they are willing to pay me, until I *know* that I can do the finest work to be found anywhere."

When Mother had her mind made up to something there wasn't much use in our trying to change it, and that was one time when I knew Grace didn't want to. She didn't say anything, but when she looked back at me she was nodding her head just the least little bit.

That two miles was about the longest two I ever walked, and Elizabeth seemed to grow heavier every time it was my turn to carry her. As the afternoon grew later a hard, dull sort of cold settled down, and before we reached the laundry Hal was stamping his feet and crying, so I had to carry him piggy-back with his feet in my coat pockets. The laundry certainly wasn't worth coming that far to see. It was an old, old one-story brick building, and I couldn't see how clean clothes could come out of any place with such dirty windows, but Mother said, "Well, one can never judge a book by its cover; it can be soiled, tattered and torn on the outside, but you may find it fascinating once you get into it."

I thought I knew Mother pretty well, but Grace knew her better than I did. While she was telling us that we must hurry right along so as to get back to Uncle Frank's before dark, Grace put her mouth close to my ear and whispered, "Do you remember how Mother used to sing on the ranch if she had to go out doors at night when the coyotes were howling? She's scared of going to work in this dirty old laundry, and the business about the book is her singing."

If Mother was scared, nobody but Grace could ever have found it out. The shortest way back to Uncle Frank's was right through the middle of the toughest neighborhood anywhere around, and, cold as it was, there were gangs of noisy young hoodlums on half a dozen of the corners we had to pass. Quite a few of them whistled at us, and a couple called Grace "Cutey," but Mother paid no more attention to them than she would have paid to so many barbers' poles. When we had passed one of the freshest gangs, Grace said to her, "If you should get a job in that particular laundry, and I hope you don't, you'd have to go the long way around and ride on the streetcar. It would be as much as your life is worth to walk through here alone and after dark."

"Oh, I shall be perfectly safe," Mother answered. "Men or boys who gather in gangs are generally cowards, and an honest woman has little to fear from them."

By the time we reached the house we were all so cold, hungry, and tired that we went to bed right after supper—even Grace.

5

Molasses on the Loose

MOTHER must have talked to Uncle Frank till long after we went to sleep that Sunday night, and she must have told him the same things she told Grace about making our living in our own home. Anyway, we three had breakfast together at six o'clock the next morning, and while we were eating he said, without leading up to it at all, "You may be right, Mary Emma, but I'm still afraid you're trying to bite off a bigger chunk than you can chew. Laundries are sweat shops, the women who work in them are the rough, coarse ones who can't find jobs anywhere else, and the bosses treat them as if they were slaves. Even if you could stand the work, the conditions would drive you out of your mind. It might be different if you were still a young girl, or if you were used to the rougher side of life, but you're not. Isn't there some other way you can learn this trade, some school or training place where you could go?"

"If there is, I've never heard of it," Mother said, "and I have no time to search for it now. Both our families need a home that is all their own, and as quickly as it can be managed. I'm not afraid of hard work, or the sort of people I may have to associate with. My life hasn't been exactly a sheltered one."

"I know, Mary Emma," Uncle Frank said, as if he were a bit irritated at her, "but . . ."

Mother didn't let him go any further, but laid a hand over on his arm. "Frank," she said, "I know you may find this hard to understand, but I think I am being led by divine guidance. This whole idea came to me suddenly when I was sitting in church yesterday, and I felt at once that a great burden had been lifted from me. I must try my level best to go through with it."

For as much as a full minute Uncle Frank sat looking down at Mother's hand, as if he were studying it. Then he laid his hand over it, looked up into her face, and said slowly, "God bless you, Mary Emma." He didn't say another word, but pushed his chair back quickly and left the table without finishing his breakfast.

It was still dark when Mother and I left the house. At the sidewalk she told me to be a good boy and not to get into any quarrels at school, then she walked away up Lawrence Street, toward the tough section of Malden. I wanted to say the same thing to her that Uncle Frank had said, but it wouldn't have sounded right, coming from me, so I just called, "Good luck, Mother," and hurried down the other way toward the store.

That Monday afternoon and evening there wasn't much business at the store, and Mr. Durant had delivered most of the coal orders before I got out of school. I suppose I could have eaten a piece of candy or two, and talked with Mr. Haushalter between customers, but I didn't want to do that. I still felt pretty good about his having paid me for the week I'd said could be a trial one, and I didn't want him to think I was slacking up just as soon as he'd told me my job would be steady. So, as soon as I'd delivered my last order, I filled a big bucket about half full of water, whittled in some yellow soap, and set it on top of the stove to heat. While I did it Mr. Haushalter was leaning on the counter, playing with Matilda, and he didn't seem to notice that I was even in the store. He was chuckling and tickling the calico cat, and she was rolling on her back and boxing at his fingers with her paws.

After I had the water on to heat, I brought the stepladder from the back room, and set it up at the far end of the store. I'd put a plank up with one end on top of the stepladder and the other on the Ivory Soap shelf, and was feeling to see if the bucket of water was getting warm when Mr. Haushalter laughed out loud. "Durned if you ain't got me beat, son," he called out. "Most generally I can keep my hair down and outwait what's goin' on, but you've got my curiosity het up to boilin'. What in Sam Hill you up to, anyways?"

I looked up at the ceiling above the stove and said, "Well, I wanted to get some of this black off, but if I just washed here above the stove it would look kind of like a white cloud in a gray sky, so I thought I'd better start washing at the back of the store. I'm not very heavy, and I think the Ivory Soap shelf is strong enough to hold me."

"Well, well, well," he said slowly. "Bless my soul if you ain't got 'em all beat. Endurin' the past thirty years John and me must have had sixty boys around here, more or less, and you're the first one to tackle an extry job without bein' told—and man-fashion to boot."

Mr. Haushalter squinted one eye and peeped over the top of his glasses at the ceiling above the stove. " 'Tis a mite black, ain't it? Must have been buildin' up for. . . . Curious, ain't it, how a little thing like that will take a man's mind back. Let . . . me . . . think. . . . Was it the fall of '79 or the spring of '80 that we bought out old man Tibbets? Well, no matter, but I recollect that ceilin' was just turnin' a trifle yellowish. The old man was pretty spry that year before; painted the whole store from clue to hearin', back room and all. Even varnished the shelves. Done it all by himself, whilst John and me took care of the trade. Must have had a notion he'd hold out for another ten years. Fine old man, Amos Tibbets. Wouldn't doubt me that paintin' spree of his had a lot to do with his passin'; heart sort of petered out on him after that."

Mr. Haushalter had gone back to playing with Matilda as he talked, but he straightened up and looked along the shelves and all around the store, with a sort of happy, far-off smile on his face. And for a little while he seemed to be talking to himself more than to me. "Ain't changed much at all," he said. "Tried to keep it just about like the old man had it; good merchant, Amos Tibbets. 'Course the brand names has changed some, and crackers comes in tin boxes 'stead o' barrels, and kerosene is up to fourteen cents a gallon, but by and all things don't change much—that is, if a man don't get took off his feet by every new notion that comes along."

My bucket of water had begun to steam, so I stood on my tiptoes, reached up over the rim, and stirred it with my finger to find out if the soap had all melted. That seemed to bring Mr. Haushalter back a little bit, and he said, "By gorry, that's the selfsame pot-bellied stove Mr. Tibbets had in the selfsame . . . No. No. He had a Franklin Burner." Then he chuckled so hard that his stomach jiggled. "Got busted up the first winter after John and me commenced business. Curious, ain't it, how a boy'll go to growin' soon's ever he gets a job in a grocery store? Growin' tall and growin' awkward. Me, I growed mostly sideways."

He chuckled again, squirted a little thin stream of tobacco juice into Matilda's sand box, and patted his stomach. "Oh, we was talkin' about stoves, wa'n't we? Well, this boy . . . first one we had . . . let me think . . . what was that boy's name? Well, no matter . . . hear he come to be a big lawyer over to New York . . . mother lives over on Myrtle Street . . . John would know his name . . . father passed away four-five years back. Well, well, no matter anyways. This boy, he growed to six foot tall that year he worked for us, and awkwarder'n an ox in a strawb'rry patch. By gorry, that just about done it. Ox? Ox? There was an ox somewheres about his name. Maddox, that was it: old Henry Maddox's boy."

Right then a woman came in for fifteen cents' worth of cheese and a pound of common crackers, so, while Mr. Haushalter was waiting on her, I took my bucket of hot water back and began washing the ceiling at one corner. It was awfully dirty, but if I got the sponge much wetter than damp the water ran down my arm, so I had to be real careful, and I forgot all about Mr. Haushalter until, from right below me, he said, "Here, this'll put an arm on you, and you'll need it for that job. By gorry, the old ceilin' was gettin' a mite dirty, wa'n't it?"

When I looked down Mr. Haushalter was holding up a slice of cheese about the size of my hand, and four common crackers. "A boy's got to eat if he's doin' a man's job," he told me. "Sit down a jiffy and get it into you whilst I tell you 'bout that Maddox boy. Don't recollect what his first name was, but that don't matter. Like I was tellin' you, he was big, and he was awkward, and he was one of the few that wa'n't lazy. Well, sir, that winter John and me got an awful good price on a hogshead of Jamaica molasses . . . used to fetch a lot of it in whenst they was distillin' Medford Rum up to the Square. It come out on a freight train from Boston—there was three or four a day in them times—and they sot it off about halfway down the platform towards the depot. As I recollect, it was an afternoon about the likes of this one; cold, with ice on the sidewalk where the eaves had dripped some along about noontime. Soon as school was out this Maddox boy, he come to work when Cop Watson and two-three others was . . ."

I had my mouth full of cheese and crackers, and I knew better than to interrupt people, but before I thought I'd asked, "The same Cop Watson that has this beat now?"

"Yep. Yep. Same one, and his feet was just as big and just as flat then as they be now, but his mustache was coal black. Well, as I was sayin', Cop Watson and two-three others was in here, standin' by the old Franklin Burner, warmin' their hands and talkin', when the Maddox boy come in. Well, just to josh him, I says, ' 'Fore you get started on somethin' else you might fetch in the hogshead o' molasses that come out on the noon train; it's on the depot platform yonder.' Then I got to listenin' to the talk and forgot all about the boy. Never had a notion he could budge that hogshead; must have weighed a good four hundred pounds. Well, sir, he did; heaved it over on its side and rolled it clean up there to the front door—there was two steps then, just like there is now, but they was different ones. How in the world he got it there without none of us seein' him I don't know, but he done it.

"First thing we seen. . . . No. No. First thing we heard was a holler out of the Maddox boy. Then Old Ned broke loose! The door come flyin' off its hinges and that hogshead o' molasses come tearin' acrost the floor towards us like it was the Portland Express. You never seen men scatter so quick in all your born days! Cop Watson, he leapt clean over the cracker barrel, I went atop the counter, and Matilda—not this one, but her great-great-great-grandmother—skun up on the top shelf yonder where we keep the lamp chimbleys."

As Mr. Haushalter had been telling the last part of the story he'd been coming closer and closer to laughing; then, when he told about the cat, he sort of exploded. He laughed so hard that his face turned scarlet. He lifted both hands above his head, and slapped them down on his thighs. "Bless my soul," he wheezed as soon as he could catch his breath, "you never seen such a goin's-on as we had here for a couple o' minutes: Franklin Burner all smashed to smithereens, stovepipe lashin' about like a caught eel, and scatterin' soot from Dan to Beersheba; apples and pickles bouncin' around like they was rubber balls, and a tableful of tinwear risin' up like a flock o' scairt ducks off'n a pond. That hogshead of molasses never slowed a mite till it fetched up amongst the flour barrels—stove one of 'em in, too."

"What happened to the Maddox boy?" I asked.

Before Mr. Haushalter could answer me he had another spell of laughing and slapping his thighs. "Oh, nothin' much," he told me between gasps. "When things had settled down a mite, I looked around, and there he sot amongst a pile o' kindlin' wood that had been the steps, both legs straight out on the floor in front of him. When he seen me look around, he says, 'I'm sorry, Gus. I slipped on the ice outside the door. You can take it out of my pay.' Lord love him, I don't recollect what we was payin' him for wages, but in them days it wouldn't a'been more'n a dollar a week—and what he could pick up around the store to eat." Mr. Haushalter stood there for a minute, chuckling to himself, then he said, "Curious, ain't it; I ain't thought of that in twenty-five years. Well, bless my soul, how time flies! Here's John a'ready with his late afternoon orders. You go on with your housecleanin', and I'll go see what luck he had."

Mr. Durant hadn't had very good luck with his late orders, and said he'd deliver them himself on his way home, so I kept on with the ceiling until half-past-six. Then, when I went to get a fresh bucket of water, Mr. Haushalter told me to knock off for the day.

When I reached Uncle Frank's house Mother hadn't come back, and we were all worried about her, so I started for the laundry at as fast a trot as I thought I could keep up all the way. I'd gone as far as the tough neighborhood when, under a street light half a block away, I saw her coming. She was walking slowly, and, for one of the few times I ever saw, with her head down. I was sure she had been hurt, or that one of the corner gangs had given her some trouble, so I ran toward her as fast as I could, shouting, "Mother, what's the matter?"

She couldn't have seen me, because I was in the middle of the block where it was dark, but before the first word was hardly out of my mouth she lifted her head and came on briskly, like a good horse that's been touched with the spurs. If I hadn't seen her before she knew I was nearby, I would never have guessed how tired she was when I reached her. The light was behind her by that time, so I couldn't see her face, but her voice sounded all full of smiles. "Why, there's nothing in the world the matter, Son," she told me. "Just the opposite, and I think your 'Good luck' this morning helped me more than anything else. I was fortunate in getting just the job I wanted, and though I'm desperately slow at it, I think they're going to keep me on. I had a nice talk with the foreman before coming away. Now tell me how things went for you at school and in the store today."

The rest of the way to Uncle Frank's house I told her about the hogshead of molasses that got away from the boy at the store, but I don't think I told her the boy's name.

6

"Pop Goes the Weasel"

I THINK my idea about washing the ceiling at the store was one of the best I ever had. We had a heavy, wet snow the day after I started it, then a cold snap, and there was hardly an hour for the rest of the week when the temperature went above zero. Whenever there was a cold snap like that we always had lots of coal orders at the store, and that week we were flooded with them. With the streets and sidewalks in frozen ridges I couldn't push the cart, and when I tried to deliver coal on a sled it tipped over so often that I spent most of my time reloading it. Besides that, my hands got so cold I couldn't hold onto the bags, and I thought my feet would freeze right off me. I didn't say anything about it at the store, but I guess Mr. Durant noticed how cold I was when I came back from my second delivery, that first morning after the freeze-up. He never talked very much, and the most he'd ever said to me was where to deliver orders, but he came over when I was trying to get my mittens off, and said, "You'd better stay here in the store with Gus, and you might work on that ceiling some more when you get a chance; it's needed it for a long time and you're doing a good job on it. Till we get a thaw, the deliveries will have to be a shoulder job, and I'll take care of it."

For a small man, and one who must have been well past fifty, Mr. Durant was the hardest worker I'd ever known. He was all business, and didn't smoke, or chew, or ever say a bad word. That week he carried out more than a hundred bags of coal, along with the grocery orders, and his hands and feet must have got just as cold as mine did, but he never stopped to warm them. He'd come in from a delivery with his face brick-red and stiff-looking from the cold, put two bags of coal on his shoulder, pick up a big basket of groceries, and go right out again. When he wasn't out collecting orders or delivering them he was busy putting them up in the store. He always moved quickly, and he was careful in everything he did. He'd never cheat a customer out of a single bean, but if he put in one too many and the beam of the scale tipped a bit above level he'd take it out.

Mr. Haushalter was just the opposite. He never hurried, he liked to talk and laugh, and tell stories, and he never took out any beans unless the scale bumped down good and hard. There was only one thing he did that might seem like cheating a customer, and he explained to me about that.

When some men chew tobacco it's a dirty habit; they're always spitting, or talking as if they had a mouthful of marbles, and some of them leak juice at the corners of their lips. Mr. Haushalter chewed all the time, but I don't believe anybody but Mr. Durant and I knew it. No one could ever have told by his talking, and he never spit when there was a customer in the store. Really, he didn't spit at all; he'd pinch his lips together and fire a squirt of brown juice as if it were a dart, and he always hit Matilda's sand box with it—sometimes from ten feet away.

Right at the beginning I thought he might be cheating the customers a little, because the first thing he'd do every morning was to take a long plug of black B-L out of the tobacco case, put it under the plug cutter, and slice off a sliver that wouldn't be more than a sixteenth of an inch thick. He noticed me watching him the second morning I worked in the store, and maybe he knew what I was thinking. Anyway, he said, "Sugar and flour and tea and coffee gets sold by the pound, and you're cheatin' a customer if you don't give him a fair tip o' the scales, but tobacca gets sold by the piece, and a piece is a piece—five cents or ten cents, accordin' to them dented lines on the plug. Now if you take note, I never shave off a sliver no thicker'n the dent line betwixt the pieces, and one sliver'll go me half a day."

It was fun working in the store with Mr. Haushalter, but I didn't get as much ceiling washed that cold week as I should have. Most people had their groceries delivered instead of coming after them, so we didn't have many customers in the store, and whenever there wasn't anyone to wait on, Mr. Haushalter would come back to talk to me. Almost every time, he'd bring me a couple of pieces of candy, or a couple of cookies, or a wedge of cheese and some crackers; then he'd tell me, "Sit you down a jiffy and get that into you, Son, whilst I tell you about. . . ." And his stories were always about things that happened years and years before I was born; things that boys who worked there had done, or about peculiar customers, or about the days when people used to bring in an egg to trade for a needle. Sometimes he'd bring an old feather duster, and putter around the shelves near where I was working. But he always told stories as he dusted, and all the good he did was to stir the dust up on one shelf so it could settle on another.

Though my job was fun, I knew that Mother's wasn't. She'd come back from the laundry at night so cold and tired she couldn't eat her supper, but if anybody said a word about it she'd get edgy, almost cross. By Saturday night she had a whole row of raw blisters on her right hand, and half a dozen burns on her left, but she acted almost like a spoiled child for a minute or two when Uncle Frank said, "Mary Emma, don't you think you've gone far enough with this foolishness? Can't you see that you're going to kill yourself if you try to go on with it?"

"I shall *not* quit," Mother said sharply. "They may let me go because I am so slow and awkward, but I shall never quit until I can do my work as rapidly and as well as the very best of those women."

When Mother began she was almost crying, but after she'd blown off steam a little she sort of wilted. "Oh, Frank," she said, "I didn't mean to be cross, and if I was it is all at myself. For years I have thought of myself as a capable, intelligent woman, but there is a colored girl who works on the bench next to mine who makes me appear as a clumsy, stupid oaf. Every garment she touches comes off her board beautifully done. The harder I try the worse I seem to do. I can't stop the constant clack, clack, clack of the machinery from getting on my nerves, and I haven't yet learned to regulate my gas-heated iron so that it won't become either too hot or too cool. Today I scorched a beautiful shirtwaist, and I'm afraid I've ruined it. If Bessie, the colored girl, hadn't insisted on putting several perfectly finished pieces over on my rack, I'm sure the foreman would have paid me off tonight."

"It's a shame he didn't," Uncle Frank told her.

"No, Frank, no," Mother answered. "I realize that it wasn't exactly honest of me to let Bessie put some of her work in with mine, but I couldn't have stopped her without hurting her feelings, and she says I will do all right as soon as my blisters heal and I get into my . . . my stride."

"Well, I still think it's foolishness for you to go on with it," Uncle Frank said, "but your friend Bessie might be right about your hitting your stride. You know, an athlete never wins a race until he learns to run relaxed; your biggest trouble might be that you're all tightened up and trying too hard. Think about the whole thing over Sunday, and if you do go back Monday morning, try taking it easier. I have a notion that might cure a lot of your troubles."

We all went to church and Sunday School the next day, just as we had the Sunday before, even to Mother's staying to talk to the minister. When we got back to the house Uncle Levi was there. He was Grandfather Gould's bachelor brother who lived in Boston, and he'd come out to see us, loaded with all the fruit and nuts and candy he could carry. From the smell of his breath and the way he acted when Mother first came in, I thought he might be loaded with something more than just fruit and candy. As soon as she opened the door he ran to her, threw his arms clear around her, and lifted her off her feet. As he hugged her he rubbed his chin into her neck and said, "By hub, Mary Emma, your old uncle's awful glad to lay eyes on you. Didn't calc'late I'd ever see you again when you and Charlie went off to Colorado. It's a God's wonder, havin' you back again with all these healthy-lookin' little shavers."

He stood her down, held her away at arm's length, and looked at her as if he were studying her face. "Curious how time gets away," he said slowly. "Here you be, a woman going on . . . forty, ain't it?"

Mother's face looked as surprised and happy as it had when she first opened the door and saw him. "Why, Uncle Levi! How did you remember?" she asked. "Yes, it will be forty in the autumn. I'm getting to be an old lady. Didn't you notice the gray that's coming into my hair?"

"House always looks homier with a little snow on the roof," he told her, "and forty ain't more'n a starter for a Gould. Father, he lived to be ninety-six. But ain't it curious how the time gets away from a body? Don't seem more'n a year or two agone since I was daddlin' you on my knee. Recollect how you used to make me sing 'Pop Goes the Weasel' and ride you on my foot? By hub, I can see you now as plain as if 'twa'n't more'n a week agone, 'stead of nigh onto forty years; no bigger'n a pint o' cider, fat cheeks blazin' red, pigtails a-flyin', and squealin' fit to kill. It's a God's wonder you didn't wear the both of us out; never did seem to know when you'd had enough."

If I'd ever seen Uncle Levi before, I couldn't remember it, and I was having so much fun listening to him that I forgot that anyone else but Mother was there until Uncle Frank said, "She don't know it any better now than she did then, Levi." He always left the "Uncle" off.

Mother could be awfully quick about heading something off if she didn't want it talked about, and she was quicker than usual that time. Before Uncle Frank had the last words out she was peeking over Uncle Levi's shoulder at him, laughing and shaking her finger as if she were playing. "Now don't you give me away, Frank," she told him. "While Uncle Levi's here we're going to have fun, and I'll bet a cookie he came just as he used to when I was a little girl on the old farm: loaded to the chin with fruit and candy."

Mother had stepped close to Uncle Levi when she peeked over his shoulder, and as soon as she'd said we were going to have fun he grabbed her in his arms and swung her around in a dance. As they started off he began to sing, " 'Round and 'round the cobbler's bench, the monkey chased the weasel, and every time the monkey jumps, *Pop* goes the weasel." Around and round they went in the middle of the parlor floor, and every time Uncle Levi sang out, "*Pop*" he'd swing Mother right up off her feet.

Mother was certainly right about our having fun while Uncle Levi was there. All afternoon, and until he went back to Boston late in the evening, he kept everybody laughing and happy. It's a wonder the younger children didn't wear him to a frazzle. If he sat down for as much as a minute, some one of them would make him cross his knees, then climb astraddle of his foot and bounce up and down as he sang "Pop Goes the Weasel." And every time he'd come to the "pop," he'd shout it and toss the rider nearly as high as his head.

Mother let all of us, except Elizabeth, stay up until Uncle Levi went home. Then, while she was helping Grace and me spread the shake-downs, she kept humming, " 'Round and 'round the cobbler's bench," and when she'd come to the "pop," she'd give an extra flip to the blanket she was spreading. When we'd finished, she said, "My, wasn't this a lovely day! It's done me more good than all the medicine in the world." I think she was right; she was still humming when she went into her room and shut the door.

That next week went fine for all of us. I finished washing the ceiling at the store and got started on the shelves. Grace found a few more odd jobs and made nearly three dollars, besides helping Aunt Hilda with the housework. The weather turned mild enough that the children could play outside part of the time, and Mother didn't seem nearly so tired when she came home from the laundry.

When we were eating supper—about Wednesday night, I think it was—she looked up at Uncle Frank and said, "My, Uncle Levi's coming did me more good than anything that's happened to me for years—and I think your telling me about the runner helped a great deal, too. So far this week I've turned out nearly as many garments as I did in all of last week, and they're beginning to have a professional look about them. Bessie has shown me so many little tricks that I never would have dreamed of. That girl is a star; she's just as kind and considerate of me as if she were my own daughter, and I suspect that she's still slipping a piece or two of her beautifully finished work over onto my rack when I'm not looking."

Then she laughed and said, "There's only one thing that's really bothering me. I've got that foolish little tune of Uncle Levi's in my head and can't get it out. I think it is the machinery that does it. All around the ceiling there are wheels and pulleys that churn out a monotonous, never-ending rhythm. Then, right above my head, there is a wheel that's at one end of a long, wide belt. Just at the moment when the "pop," in the song comes along, the splice on that belt pops as it goes over the wheel. Before six o'clock came tonight, I thought it would drive me frantic. I must learn to sing spirituals while I work, the way Bessie does, so as to break that terribly monotonous rhythm."

Then she looked over at Grace and asked, "Gracie, have you had any further chance to look for a house for us? If I'm able to keep on improving as rapidly as I have this week, it won't be too long before we could think about starting a little business of our own. Bessie tells me the laundry charges twenty-five cents apiece for fancy shirtwaists, and I did up seventeen of them today. If we could get prices like that, and I could pick up my speed a little, I think we could afford to pay as much as twelve or thirteen dollars a month for rent. Let's see, it was seven we paid in Colorado, wasn't it?"

"Mmm, hmm," Grace said, "but the only one I've seen that would be big enough, and wouldn't cost nearly twenty dollars, is down by the brickyards. We wouldn't have to live in it forever, and we wouldn't have to be like those people down there just because we lived among them."

"No!" Mother said. "No! I will not do it! If necessary, I'll stay right in that laundry until I can turn out enough work that we can afford twenty dollars a month, but I will not have our home in that neighborhood. Now you run along and take care of Mrs. Benk's dishes; I'll help Aunt Hilda with ours."

Right behind the tobacco case at the store there was an old roll-topped desk with rows of little pigeonholes where the charge-account pads were kept; most of the delivery orders were charge-it, and so was about half of the business from people who came into the store. The last thing every night, Mr.

Durant sat down at the desk, added whatever had been bought during the day onto the pads, and then totaled them. He never looked up from the desk when he was working on the pads, and, right at the beginning, Mr. Haushalter had told me I must never disturb him. I did it the Friday night of that week without meaning to.

As soon as I came in from school I started washing the top shelf, way at the back end of the store; moving things as I went along, then putting them back as soon as I had that section of the shelf washed and dried. By half-past-six I'd finished all but the last section—the one where we kept the lamp chimneys, right beside Mr. Durant's desk. I moved the stepladder in beside the desk real carefully, so that I didn't make any noise, and then climbed up to move the chimneys. The ladder must have teetered a little, or I must have slipped. Anyway, I almost lost my balance, and in grabbing hold of the shelf I knocked a lamp chimney down. It broke into a thousand pieces on the high top of the desk, and chips of glass showered all over Mr. Durant and the pads. He ducked, then looked up quick, and I was sure he was going to scold me, but he just asked, "How is your mother getting along?"

I guess it was because I was a little bit nervous, but after I got started talking there didn't seem to be any place to stop. I told him about her working in the laundry so she could learn how to do up fancy shirtwaists worth twenty-five cents apiece, and about Bessie helping her, and about her saying she wouldn't let us live down by the brickyards, and about second-hand furniture being so high. I don't remember all that I did tell him, but I couldn't seem to get stopped until he told me to sweep up the glass while he finished his bookkeeping. Maybe it was because I talked so long that he forgot to, but he never did scold me for breaking the lamp chimney.

All the way home from the store that night I was ashamed of myself; not so much for breaking the chimney as for not knowing when to stop talking, but I think it worked out good instead of bad. When I came in from making a delivery Saturday afternoon Mr. Durant was putting up an order, but he called me over to him. "Could your mother pay fifteen dollars rent?" he asked me.

"Well, she said she could afford to pay twelve or thirteen. I guess we could go as much as fifteen if we had to," I told him.

"Do you know the big gray house down the street, next to the fire station?" he asked as he watched the scale beam and sifted a few more grains of sugar into the bag.

"The one where Mr. La Plante, the fireman, lives upstairs?" I asked him.

Without taking his eyes away from the beam, he nodded and said, "Folks downstairs are being evicted at the end of the month. Your mother might get that for fifteen; not less. And at that price the owner wouldn't spend any money to fix it up. But there is a big room at the back of the cellar; might work out for a laundry room. Tell your mother I'll speak to the owner if she wants. There are extra bedrooms in the attic. Whole place will be dirty, but it appears you're pretty good at scrubbing, and wallpaper's cheap."

On Saturday nights I worked till nine o'clock, and Mother wasn't home from the laundry when I went to Uncle Frank's for supper, so I didn't have any chance to tell her about the house until just before I went to bed. But Sunday morning she and Grace and I went to look at it before Sunday School time. Of course we could only look at it from the outside. The downstairs windows were dirty, and there were no shades at them, but the second floor and the outside of the house and the yard looked fine.

We walked past three or four times, and it was easy to see that Mother wanted the house right from the first. "Oh, my!" she said when I pointed it out to her. "Regardless of the rent, we could never afford it. Why, at the prices they're asking for. used furniture, we couldn't begin to furnish it."

"Well, we could furnish one or two rooms to begin with, couldn't we?" Grace asked. "Then, as we made some money, we could furnish the others, one at a time. We could get along all right for a while with just a stove, and a table or two, and some chairs, and a few more bedclothes."

"I suppose we could," Mother said slowly, "but it would be a big undertaking, and we have no definite assurance that we could find enough customers to make more than a bare living

. . . although Mr. Vander Mark tells me he has spoken to several of the well-to-do parishioners at our church and they'd like to see samples of my work."

"Then let's take it," Grace said as we turned to walk past the house again.

"Let's not be hasty," Mother told her. "We're far from out of the woods yet. The amount I make in the laundry would barely pay our grocery bill, and you and Ralph together are making scarcely more than the fifteen dollars it would take for rent alone."

"That's just for right now," I told her. "When school vacation time comes I'll make twice as much. And then, too, if I get up bright and early in the mornings I could carry a paper route before I go to work in the store."

"Oh, Son, you're always so impulsive!" Mother said, almost as if she were scolding me. "I know how hard all you children would work to help out, but I shall not let us get into anything where there will be need for you to work beyond your strength, or where we'll have to dip into what there is left of our money for ordinary living expenses."

As she spoke, Mother had been looking at the other houses along the street, and at the James School, next to the fire station. "I should love to think that we might have this nice big house, in this good neighborhood and right close to the children's school, but it seems to me that it is way beyond our means right now; it would take a fabulous amount to ever furnish it properly."

When Grace kept quiet during any argument it was because she was thinking, and the longer she kept still the better job of thinking she usually did. She did a pretty good job that time. Without looking up from the sidewalk, and without seeming to be talking to anybody, she said, "Trust in the Lord and do. . . ."

Mother didn't let her finish. She just said to me quickly, "Tell Mr. Durant I should be glad to have him speak to the landlord. We must hurry or you children will be late for Sunday School."

7

A Pretty Reasonable Fellow

WITH us, good luck and bad luck always seemed to come in waves, and we seemed to be right in the middle of a good-luck wave. On Monday Mr. Durant talked to the owner of the big house on Spring Street and got it for us. On Tuesday morning Mother gave me the first month's rent before she went to work, and I took it to Mrs. Perkins, the landlord's wife, when I went to deliver her groceries.

Then, on Wednesday night, I sat up and played cribbage with Uncle Frank until nearly ten o'clock. After we'd finished he picked up the paper and read it as I made up my bed on the floor. I was all ready to crawl into it when he called to Mother, "Mary Emma, this might be a chance for you to pick up some furniture. Old Grandma Maddox, over on Myrtle Street, died yesterday, and they're going to have the funeral Friday. Her son's coming down from New York, but I don't have a notion he'll want to ship the stuff back there. He might sell it for a pretty reasonable price."

"Did Mrs. Maddox have a nice home?" Mother asked.

"Looked nice and neat from the outside," Uncle Frank answered, "but I was never in it. I expect the stuff is pretty old-fashioned; Grandma must have been in her nineties."

"I'm afraid her things would be too expensive for us, Frank," Mother called back from the kitchen. "We're going to start off with just as little as we can, then add to it as we go along."

"Well, you might find this Maddox a pretty reasonable fellow," Uncle Frank called back. "It says here that he's a big lawyer, and the bigger they are the harder they fall."

The second he said "big lawyer," it was as if somebody had turned on a light in my head. I jumped up and called out, "I know him!" Then I remembered that I didn't, but I was sure he must be the same Maddox boy that let the hogshead of molasses get away from him in the grocery store. I started to tell the whole story to Uncle Frank, but Mother called, "Some other time, Son! You'll have to be up early in the morning and it's time you were asleep."

I was up good and early the next morning, and while Mother was getting breakfast and Uncle Frank was shaving I found the piece he'd been reading in the paper, cut it out and put it in my pocket. As soon as I got down to the store I showed it to Mr. Haushalter and asked him if the lawyer wasn't the same boy who used to work in the store.

"Well, well, well! Bless my soul!" he said when he'd read it. "Couldn't be no other but him. Richard. Richard. Now ain't it curious I couldn't think of his first name. But come to think of it, nobody never called him that around here; he was always Dickie, Dickie Maddox. Well, well, well. Ain't seen or heard tell of him in twenty-five years."

Mr. Haushalter had just put his morning's sliver of tobacco in his mouth when I took the piece of paper from him. He sort of gathered the quid together with his tongue, rolled it over a couple of times, and poked it away in his cheek. "Poor old Grandma Maddox, passed on and gone," he said in a sorrowful voice. Then he gave the chew another little poke with his tongue, and said, "Don't know why I said that anyways. Kind of expect the poor old soul was sort o' glad to go. Expect lots of 'em is glad to go when their time comes. Old lady hadn't took much interest in life since Henry passed on—he was her husband; Dickie's pa. Don't calcalate Dickie'll stay on 'ceptin' to close up the house and maybe sell it."

"Do you think Mr. Maddox would sell the furniture?" I asked.

"Lord love you, 'course he'd sell it! What else would he do with it? Don't have a notion there's a stick of it less'n sixty years old. What would a big lawyer like him want with old stuff the likes of that?"

"I know," I said, "but I meant at a price somebody could afford to pay."

"Oh, I don't expect he'd want all outdoors for it, why?"

"Well," I said, "you know we rented the big house next to the fire station, beginning the first of the month, and we haven't any furniture for it, and . . ."

"Well, bless my soul, if I ain't gettin' simpler minded by the year! 'Course you need furniture! Now what was the matter with my head that I didn't think about it? And there ain't no reason Dickie Maddox couldn't sell the old lady's stuff for most anything he was offered. Let me see . . . let me see. Funeral's goin' to be up to the Baptist Church at ten o'clock, ain't it? If things was so I could get away from the store tomorrow mornin' . . ."

"I could take care of the store for you," I told him. "Mother will always write me a note if I have to stay out of school for something important."

"Hmmmm, hmmmm. Don't doubt me you could do it for a couple of hours in a pinch; how many beans in a quart?"

"A pound and fourteen ounces," I told him.

"How much is kerosene?"

"Fourteen cents a gallon, but eight cents for half a gallon," I said.

"Well, well, well. Learnin' fast, ain't you? Best to get on with washin' them windows; time's a-flyin'. Just might happen I'll take in old Grandma Maddox's funeral—ain't seen or heard tell of Dickie in more'n twenty-five years—don't have a notion he'd remember me noways. I'll think 'bout it endurin the day and leave you know before you go home tonight."

I think Mr. Haushalter wanted to talk to Mr. Durant before he said it would be all right for me to tend store while he went to Mrs. Maddox's funeral, but just before we locked up that night he told me, "If your ma's agreeable to you stayin' out of school in the forenoon tomorrow, I don't know but what I'd take in old Grandma Maddox's funeral. 'Course I'd come down and get you started off in good shape before I went, and haply I wouldn't go out to the buryin' grounds at all; that way I'd prob'ly be back well afore noontime."

I told him I'd tell Mother, and that I was sure she'd say it would be all right. Then, when I was nearly up to Uebel's drug store, he called me back and told me, "Now don't say nothin' 'bout the old lady's furniture; a man's in bad business when he counts his chickens afore he's put the hen a-settin'."

I was waiting outside the store door when Mr. Haushalter got there the next morning. He was a few minutes late, but he was all dressed up in a blue serge suit and a white shirt, and he had his shoes shined till they sparkled in the light from the street lamp. The suit was one I think he must have had for a long, long time; the lapels of the coat were wide but no longer than my hand, it buttoned right up to the knot of his tie, and it was tight enough around the middle that there were scallops between the buttons. After he'd unlocked the doors and the cash drawer under the counter, he only fed Matilda and looked at her kittens. Then he kept away from things that might get his suit dirty and told me how to get the fire going good, and things I'd need to know while he was away.

I think Mr. Haushalter and I were both kind of anxious for the funeral time to come. He kept walking up and down the length of the store, as if he didn't know what to do with himself, and I wanted to have as much time as I could to run the store alone before Mr. Durant would get in with his morning orders. On just about every other trip Mr. Haushalter made up and down the floor, he'd think of something else he should have told me.

Of course, I don't remember them all, but one time he stopped and told me, "Now it's all right to charge stuff to most of the folks that comes in here, but there is them that you'll have to fight shy of, and seein' you alone in the store they'd be just the ones that might come in and get a raft of stuff charged. You know the Smitherses, in the house you folks has rented; well, them. And then there's the Foxes—not the ones on Washington Street, but the ones down by the brickyards. If any of them comes in, just tell 'em it'll have to be for cash before you fetch out the stuff. Oh, yes, that littlest Jacobs boy; if you have to get him kerosene or somethin'-or-other out of the back room, he'll snitch an orange if you don't keep an eye on him."

It was about half-past-nine when Mr. Haushalter left for the funeral, and I'd made up my mind that while he was gone I'd do things just the way he always did them. The first thing I did was to go to the tobacco case, get out the long plug of black B-L, and slice off a sliver exactly the width of the dent mark. Then I folded it four times before I put it into my mouth, just the way Mr. Haushalter did. I'd barely started gathering it into a quid with my tongue when Miss Heath, my Sunday School teacher, came in for a gallon of kerosene.

If I hadn't known her, or if she'd just said, "A gallon of kerosene, please," I'd have been all right, I think. But she didn't. As she came down the two steps inside the door she sang out, "Isn't this a lovely morning? Do you have mornings like this in Colorado?"

I managed to say "Yes'm," sort of around the chew, without having any trouble. And I got by pretty well when she asked if I was tending the store all alone. But when she asked me why Mr. Haushalter wasn't there and where he'd gone, I was licked. There were only two things I could do: either run the risk of having the chew fall out of my mouth if I tried to talk around it, or swallow it. I swallowed it. But it didn't stay down more than ten seconds after I'd got hold of Miss Heath's kerosene can and escaped into the back room. And I didn't feel a bit well when I took the can back to her and asked, "Charge it?"

Miss Heath seemed to be nearly as shaken up as I felt, and she looked at me as if she were terribly worried. "What happened to you?" she asked. "Did you hurt yourself? Why, you're as white as a pillow case, and I thought I heard a sound as if you were crying back there."

My stomach felt as if it were on fire, and my mouth was almost running over with the saliva that kept pouring into it, but I managed to say, "No, ma'am, I just got a little dizzy spell for a minute, but I'm all right now."

I had to answer four or five more questions—and hope I wouldn't be sick again—before she went out, saying she must talk to Mother about my having dizzy spells.

From the minute Mr. Haushalter had mentioned letting me tend the store alone I'd been hoping I'd have lots of customers, so I could show both them and him what a good job I could do. After Miss Heath went out I didn't want to see anybody—or have anybody see me—but it didn't work that way. Half of the women in the neighborhood must have come in, and every one of them chattered like a blue jay; asking me if I didn't feel well, and where Mr. Haushalter was, and if it wasn't a lovely morning.

For me it wasn't. My stomach still felt as if there were a fire in it, the water ran into my mouth so fast that I had to swallow every time I tried to answer a woman's question, and the swallowing gave me the hiccups. I could usually stop hiccups by taking nine swallows of water without catching my breath, but I was already swallowing more water than I could handle, so I decided to try cold buttermilk. It would always soothe sunburn for me, or the stinging burn of poison ivy, so I tried it, but it wasn't any good for that tobacco burn in my stomach, or the hiccups either.

The big icebox was in the back room, and we kept the two-gallon can of buttermilk right in the compartment with the ice, so it was always good and cold. The first excuse I could find for going back there, I opened the ice compartment door, tipped the can down, and tried to take nine big swallows without catching my breath. It might have worked all right if I hadn't had a hiccup right in the middle of the fifth swallow. It came so quick and so unexpected that I didn't have any chance to tip the can up, and buttermilk ran down the sides of my cheeks and my neck and into my shirt. As soon as I'd stopped being sick I wiped out as much of the buttermilk as I could reach with my handkerchief, but I didn't get it all, and it didn't smell very good.

Mother had taught us all that it was wicked to lie, but I just had to lie to those women that morning. I couldn't tell them what had started all the trouble, and I didn't want them to know I was being sick, so I just told the different ones anything that came into my head, and I don't think very many of them believed me. The longer that buttermilk was down inside my shirt the worse it smelled, and my mouth tasted even worse than that. As I got a chance, I tried a piece of peppermint candy, and some Blackjack gum, and even a bite of a raw onion, but they all turned out bad instead of good. And, before Mr. Durant came in with his morning orders, I'd promised myself a thousand times that I'd never try to chew tobacco again.

When Mr. Durant did come in I stayed as far away from him as I could, and if I was still looking a little puny he didn't seem to notice it. After he'd asked me how business was, he went right to work on putting up his orders. Then, when twelve o'clock came and Mr. Haushalter wasn't back, he told me to run along and get my lunch while he tended store. About the last thing in the world that I wanted was lunch, so I told him that I wasn't hungry and would wait till Mr. Haushalter came back, but he pushed some packages together on the counter and said, "No, you run along. Your aunt ordered this stuff and I told her I'd send it by you at noontime."

I hated to go back to Uncle Frank's house that noon, smelling and feeling the way I did, but there was nothing else I could do. I wasn't so much worried about Aunt Hilda, but Grace was as nosy as a hound dog, and her smeller was just about as good. Before I left the store I bit good and deep into an onion, and I chewed a piece of licorice all the way to the house, but I don't

think I fooled Grace at all. She could always ask the kind
of questions that would catch me if I was lying, and she caught
me two or three times while I was trying to explain why I was
pale and didn't want any lunch. She didn't come right out and
tell me that I'd never go to heaven, but all the time she was
washing the dishes she kept singing a church hymn about
"Someone will knock at the pearly gates, by-yye and bye, by-yye
and bye; hear a voice saying, 'I know you not,' by-byye and bye,
by-yye and bye." It got on my nerves so much that the tune
kept going over and over in my head all the rest of the day.

It was nearly two o'clock before Mr. Haushalter came back
from the funeral, and there wasn't any sense in my going to
school for only an hour and a half, so I stayed at the store with
him, but he wouldn't say a word about furniture. When I asked
him if he'd had any chance to talk to Mr. Maddox, he said,
"Why, bless your soul, I talked to him more'n ary other one that
was to the funeral. Knowed me right off the reel. Even had me
ride out to the buryin' grounds and back in the same carriage
with him."

"Did you get a chance to ask him if . . . ?"

Mr. Haushalter chuckled and asked, " 'Bout recollectin' the
time the hogshead of molasses got away from him? Lord love
you, no! I couldn't a-stirred that up again without laughin', and
it wa'n't the right thing to do at a funeral. But, by gorry, he
recollects folks that hadn't crossed my memory in a score o'
years; folks that used to live hereabouts and has passed on or
moved away. Well, well well, 'twas a right nice funeral; lots of
folks there. It's a pity old Grandma couldn't have saw the nice
turn-out for her . . . and all the flowers. Bless my soul, the
whole altar of the church was piled with 'em, smelt like a. . . ."
Then he sniffed and said, "Kind of a curious smell hereabouts;
spill somethin'?"

"Yes, sir," I told him, "a little buttermilk spilled on me. Maybe
that's what you smell." Then I stayed away from him as much
as I could for the rest of the afternoon, delivering orders and
washing shelves in the back end of the store.

It took Mr. Haushalter so long to tell everybody who came

in about the funeral that he didn't have time to say any more to me until closing time. Then, as he was locking the door, he said, "Oh, by the way, you might tell your ma to go over to Maddoxs' house after supper, 'long about eight o'clock. Dickie, he'll be there and a-lookin' out for her. Tell her not to make him no offer, and there won't be no need for her to tell him she's a widow woman, or about you children; just say she'd be willin' to take everything in the house off'n his hands—lock, stock and barrel—and let him set his own price on what he wants for it. Tell her there ain't no call to be scairt; Dickie, he's turned out to be a fine man and he won't rob her none."

Mother was scared, though. Everybody was at the table when I came in from work, and I told her what Mr. Haushalter had said right away, but it upset her so much she couldn't eat the rest of her supper. When I'd finished she said to Uncle Frank, "Why, I could only make myself ridiculous by doing a thing like that! If that house is nicely furnished—even if the things are somewhat old—the amount of money we could afford to spend right now wouldn't make a drop in the pail. Just imagine me walking in there with only a hundred and fifty dollars to my name and telling that man I wanted to buy everything in his house! Why, it would be preposterous!"

Then she turned to me and said, "No, Son. Right after supper you must go over there and tell Mr. Maddox . . ."

"Now wait a minute, Mary Emma," Uncle Frank cut in, "a hundred and fifty might go a good ways toward buying that furniture if he wants to get rid of it in a hurry, and Hilda and I could scrape up a few dollars to . . ."

"No, Frank! No!" Mother told him. "You and Hilda have all you can do to take care of your own family, and we are *not* going to start leaning on our relatives. We'll buy our furniture piece by piece, as we can afford it."

"All right! All right!" Uncle Frank said, a little bit irritably. "But don't kick the pail over till you know what's in it. There's no need of going at this exactly as Gus Haushalter said. You might be able to buy the pieces you do need and can afford at a pretty good bargain. Then too, if this man Maddox is as well-off as Gus seems to think, he isn't going to be too hungry for all of the money right away. He might be glad to take a hundred or so down, then let you pay the rest of it out over the next year or two. If you don't want to go, why not let me go over and have a talk with him?"

Mother pinched her lips together for a minute, and then said, "No, Frank, I'll go myself, but you may be sure that if I buy anything, it will be only such pieces as we can afford to pay cash for; we are *not* going into debt."

From then until eight o'clock Mother was so nervous she could hardly sit still, and when she went out she looked as if she felt the way I used to when I had to take a note home from school that I was sure would get me a spanking. She was gone for more than an hour, and when she came back she was so excited she could neither talk like herself nor stop talking. She seemed to be halfway between laughing and crying when she opened the door, and her voice went all squeaky when she called, "Frank, Hilda, children, you never saw anything like it in all your lives! That house is furnished from cellar to garret with the loveliest old walnut furniture that I've seen in years and years: dressers with acorn handles and marble tops, gate-legged tables and tapestry-seated chairs, four-poster beds and a beautiful square-grand piano, and I've bought every stick and stiver of it for fifty dollars—rugs, bed clothing, and even the dishes and dishtowels. Oh, let me catch my breath a minute before I tell you the rest of it; I've run almost every step of the way back."

She wiped a tear out of the corner of each eye and sat panting for a minute, then she turned to me with a real sober look on her face and asked, "Did Mr. Haushalter tell Mr. Maddox that Father wasn't living and that we had very little money with which to buy furniture?"

"No, ma'am, I'm sure he didn't," I told her. "He said they talked about people who used to live around here thirty years ago."

"Well," Mother said, "there is something very strange about this. Come to think of it, I don't believe I bought that furniture at all; I think he sold it to me—or rather, came as close to giving it to me as he could and save my pride. And I don't think I thanked him adequately for it. I was so excited that I could only think of getting back and telling you children about it. Just think of it! Less than a month ago I was afraid we might be ruined, and now, within a week or ten days at the most, we shall have the sort of a home that I've dreamed of having ever since I was a little girl."

She had to stop a minute to keep herself from crying. Then she went on, "And within a month, if all goes well, I should have learned enough about the laundry business that we can strike out for ourselves. Now run along to bed, children; it's getting late and you all need your rest."

8

A Bigger Chunk than We Can Chew

During the past week I think everything had gone pretty well for Mother at the laundry. At least she hadn't seemed nearly so tired when she came back at night. Her blisters had all healed, and I heard her tell Aunt Hilda that all she needed before she'd feel safe in starting her own business was a few more weeks of experience. Then, right after she bought the furniture, her nerves went all to pieces.

Maybe knowing that we'd soon be able to move into our own home made her over-anxious, so that she tried to push herself too hard in getting the experience she wanted, or maybe it was just the waiting. Whatever it was, it hit her hard and quick. Monday night little things that she wouldn't usually have noticed irritated her. Tuesday night she snapped at any one of us who made the least bit of noise, and Wednesday night she nearly exploded when Hal dropped a spoon at the supper table.

"Now look here, Mary Emma, you've reached the end of your rope," Uncle Frank told her. "This business of trying to work at

slave labor for ten hours a day, then walking two miles on top
of it, is going to kill you. If you want to live to raise these children you'd better quit it, and *right now*."

From the sharp way Mother looked at Uncle Frank I was
sure she was going to scold back at him. She almost glared for a
few seconds, then the wind suddenly went out of her sail, and
she was close to the edge of crying when she said, "It's not the
work . . . or the walking; that doesn't bother me any more. It's
that confounded song of Uncle Levi's! All day long, that big
wheel above my head keeps up its infernal chant of, 'round and
round the cobbler's bench,' then the splice on the belt comes
along and shouts, '*Pop* goes the weasel.' I thought it would drive
me frantic before six o'clock came tonight."

Uncle Frank pushed his chair back, came around the table,
and hugged Mother's head against him till she was breathing
easy again. Then he said, "Come on, Mary Emma, get your coat.
You and I are going for a little walk."

Of course, I don't know what they said to each other while
they were out walking, but when they came back Mother was
smiling and happy. "It's all over, children," she told us as she
came in. "I'm not going back to work in the laundry again, and
I'm not going to be crotchety any more. We'll move into our
house the minute the present tenants move out, and I'm going
to stop worrying about what might happen to us. With the
Lord's help we've been able to make ourselves a good living
ever since Father died, and the fortune that has befallen us
here in Medford certainly doesn't lead me to believe we will be
abandoned now."

Mother wasn't exactly right when she said we'd move into
the house the minute the other tenants moved out, but she was
pretty close. Late in the afternoon of January thirty-first the
sheriff's van came and moved the Smitherses out. Mr. Durant
brought me the keys when he came in from his last delivery,
and right after supper Mother, Grace and I went to look the
house over. Before we could see anything I had to light matches
and hunt around in the cellar for the gas meter. It was the kind

that you had to put a quarter into, and that would shut off the gas when the quarter's worth had been used up. The Smitherses must not have put a quarter in for a long time; there wasn't enough gas left in the pipes to make a flicker.

Even though Mr. Durant never did any gossiping, he knew more about the people in our end of Medford, and how they lived, than anyone else—unless it was Cop Watson. And he was right when he told me that the whole house would be dirty. It was worse than that; it was filthy. Mr. Haushalter had told me that both Mr. and Mrs. Smithers were drunk half the time, and that their children were a disgrace to the neighborhood. They must have lived like pigs. The walls were gouged and marked up with crayons, the windows and woodwork were a mess, and I don't think the floors had been scrubbed in years.

When I'd put a quarter in the meter and was able to light the gas Mother looked around with a shocked expression on her face. "Why," she said, "I never saw such a filthy sty in all my life! Even a hog will keep one corner of its pen clean! Good heavens! I wouldn't think for a moment of putting that lovely furniture into any such place as this!"

Mother stood for several minutes, looking all around with her lips pinched tight together, then she turned to Grace and said, "Well, I don't suppose there is anything that wallpaper, soap and hot water won't cure, but there's an awful lot of work to be done here before we can think of moving in. We'll have to get at it bright and early in the morning."

We were standing in the kitchen when I'd lighted the first gas jet. After Mother had finished talking to Grace, she asked, "Son, did you bring plenty of matches? If you did we'll light the gas in the other rooms and see what might be done with them."

Old and dirty as the house was, it was exactly what we needed. It was a great big, two-and-a-half story house that had been built in the 1850's for a single family. But when our landlord had bought it he had divided it, making a flat on the second floor, where the La Plantes lived. On the ground floor there were four big rooms that had been built for a front parlor, a living room, a dining room and a kitchen. On the third floor there were three bedrooms, all with dormer windows and part of the ceiling slanting down with the roof. Inside the front door there was a big square hall, with a winding staircase to the second floor, then a narrower one to the third.

The land sloped down from the street, so that the kitchen steps had to be high, then leveled off into a big yard that was a full story lower than the ground floor. The whole back half of the cellar had once been servants' quarters, with good floors, three windows along each side, and a bathroom that was set back into the space left for a cellar. The tub and basin were made of tin, but that didn't make any difference to us, because we'd never had a bathroom before.

At some time, the inside walls of the servants' quarters had been torn down, leaving a single room the width of the whole house and more than half its length. At the back of it there was a hallway, with a door that opened level with the back yard, and a stairway that led up to the kitchen. In the cellar itself there were bins that would have held twenty tons of coal, and a furnace big enough to have burned it all in a single winter.

After we had gone all through our part of the house Grace was almost dancing, and Mother had either become used to the dirt or was so pleased that she was willing to overlook it. She led us back to the big room in the basement, stood in the middle of it and, after looking it all over again, said, "Won't this be ideal for our business, Gracie? We could have a row of set tubs along those windows at the north, and our ironing boards on the sunny side. No better place could be found for drying clothes in summer than that big back yard. Then, with our having this lovely furnace, the whole cellar could be turned into a wonderful winter drying room. Oh, my! I'm letting my enthusiasm run away with me. With this house so dirty, it will be another week or more before we can possibly get it cleaned up and move in."

"I don't think so," Grace told her. "In the beginning we were talking about furnishing the house, room by room, as we could afford it. Just because we were lucky enough to get the furniture all at once I don't see any reason for changing our minds. We'll need hot water to clean with, and to heat it we'll need a stove, so the kitchen is the place we'll have to start. As soon as it's cleaned and papered and painted, we'll have a place to cook and eat. Then we could scrub that big room off the dining room, move in a bed and dresser, and make it into a bedroom for you and Elizabeth. The rest of us can sleep on shake-downs, and we could paint and paper it later. If we can get the kitchen stove moved in tomorrow morning I don't see why we couldn't be living here by day after tomorrow night."

"Oh, my!" Mother said. "It seems to me that . . . that, as Uncle Frank would say, you're trying to bite off a bigger chunk than we can chew. But you're right about our needing a stove before we can do much cleaning. I'll speak to Uncle Frank about finding a man who does such work as moving. Ralph, you might wait until Gracie and I go up to the kitchen, then turn out the gas down here. We can do nothing here tonight, and with a big day ahead of us you children must have your rest."

Before I left the store for school the next morning I saw Fritz Young drive past with a kitchen stove on his dumpcart, and a few minutes later Mother and Grace went by with pails full of rags and brushes. By the time I got out of school for lunch our kitchen looked ten times as bad as it had when we first saw it. Mr. Young had knocked a lot of soot out of the chimney when he set up the stove, and Grace and Mother had stripped down wallpaper until it lay in windrows. There had been so many layers that they'd had to soak it to get it off, and puddles of dirty water were standing on the floor between the windrows.

"Don't stand there gawking," Grace snapped at me when I'd opened the door and was looking in. "Get a basket or a box and start lugging some of this rubbish out!"

"No," Mother said quickly, "you'd get your school clothes dirty the first thing you did, and I will not have you going to school dirty. Suppose you run up to the store and get us a pound of common crackers and half a pound of cheese. And some tea," she added. "You might get a whole pound of tea—the better grade—we'll need it to hold us together at this sort of work. You'll find the money in my purse, right over. . . . Gracie, where did I lay my purse?"

Grace was peeling paper off with an old kitchen knife. She didn't look around, but said, "You didn't bring it."

"That doesn't make any difference," I told Mother. "At our store most everything is charged. I'll just tell Mr. Haushalter to put it on a pad for us."

"Not a bit of it!" Mother said almost crossly. "We're not going to run up any grocery bill until we know where the money's coming from to pay it. First you go and ask Aunt Hilda to give you a dollar out of my purse; that should cover it."

"I'll only need eighty-two cents," I told her. "The best mixed tea is sixty cents a pound, and a half a pound of cheese is ten, and . . ."

"Never mind that now," she told me, "but hurry right along. I can't have you being late for school just because we have a little extra work on our hands."

When I was halfway down the steps she called me back and said, "We're not going to get into the habit of borrowing things, but you might ask Mr. Haushalter if we could use his step-ladder for the rest of the day. I forgot to ask Mr. Young to bring the one from the Maddox house."

I'd kind of hoped I could get my clothes just a little bit dirty, so Mother wouldn't make me go to school in the afternoon, but I didn't have a chance. Aunt Hilda made me eat some lunch before I went to the store, and by the time I got back to the house it was too late. I had to run all the way to get into class before the last bell rang.

I went right to the store after school, changed into the overalls and blue shirt I wore when I had dirty jobs to do, and was washing shelves when Mr. Durant came in with the afternoon orders. He motioned me over to him while he was putting them up and told me, "You can let those shelves go for now. Till your

mother gets that house in shape you can hustle out the afternoon orders and then knock off for the day; she needs your
scrubbing more than we do right now. If you want, you can
ride the bicycle; sidewalks are getting in pretty good shape
again."

Before five o'clock I had the last delivery made and Mr.
Durant told me to run along. When I got to our house the
kitchen walls were stripped as bare as a picked chicken. Mother
was washing woodwork and Grace was scraping the last rem-
nants of paper off the ceiling. As I opened the door she was
saying to Mother, "Hadn't you better stop now if you're going
to Medford Square before the paint store closes? Unless we
have paper and paste tonight, we'll never be ready to move into
this kitchen tomorrow. I don't know how many rolls it will take,
but the ceiling is two hundred and eighty square feet, and the
walls four hundred and eighty—after allowing for the doors and
windows. Do you think one quart of paint will be enough for
the woodwork? And we'll need a paintbrush."

It sounded to me as if that much paper and paste and other
things would be more than Mother could handle, so I asked,
"Hadn't I better go along and help you carry it, Mother?"

As I looked up to ask, Grace was standing on the stepladder
above Mother. She scowled down at me and shook her head
hard, then nodded it when Mother said, "Oh, I think I shall be
able to manage it all right, Son. It would help more if you could
get this mess on the floor cleared up while I'm gone."

As soon as Mother was down the steps I asked Grace, "What's
the matter with you anyway? Don't you know that you told
Mother to bring more stuff than a stout mule could carry? Why
were you shaking your head when I asked if I could go along
to help her?"

"Don't be a ninny!" she told me. "If you went with her she'd
have to walk both ways, because there wouldn't be any more
than the two of you could carry. This way she won't have to
walk home or carry anything. The paint man will bring her back
in his delivery wagon. I know he's got one, because it went past

Uncle Frank's house just the other day. Now hurry up and get that floor cleaned; you'll have to go somewhere and find me some long boards and a couple of boxes to make a table out of. Wallpaper has to be pasted on the back, and we'll need a long table to do it on."

9

Not a Bit Professional

GRACE had been right when she sent Mother off after the paper alone. I'd barely finished cleaning the floor, and hadn't had any chance to go hunting for boards and boxes, when the paint man brought Mother home. And besides bringing the things Grace had told her to get, he brought a long folding table and several different kinds of brushes, a knife with a little curved blade, and a couple of smoothing wheels. "You can keep these till you're finished with your paper-hanging," he told Mother. Then he asked, "You've hung it before, haven't you?"

Mother smiled and said, "I've helped my husband with it several times, and am sure we won't have any trouble." Then she thanked him for bringing her home and for offering to let us use his table and tools.

As soon as he had gone she rubbed her hand over the smooth table top, and said, "Wasn't it nice of Mr. Evans to offer us the use of all his professional equipment? My! This will certainly make our task much easier! I was worried about our trying to put up wallpaper without the proper things to do it with. While I'm changing my clothes, Gracie, you might whack up some sandwiches and put water on to boil for tea. I think we'd better eat before we tackle this papering job; we won't want to stop right in the middle of it."

It's a good thing we did eat first, and that Mother let both Grace and me have tea with our sandwiches. And when she said, "tackle this papering job," she picked just the right words. While we were eating, Mother and Grace decided that we'd better start with the ceiling. Then they talked about whether it would be better to trim the edges off the paper and butt it, or whether it would be best to overlap it. At last Mother said, "Let's overlap it. The design is watered silk, so the overlaps won't show badly. We must remember that we're not experts at paper-hanging, and if we should fail to trim the edges exactly even we might have a little difficulty in making the strips butt together nicely. Well, let's clear things up here and get started; I'm anxious to see how it's going to look.

"Gracie, I'll do the measuring, we'll let Ralph paint the paste on, and you may do the actual hanging; you're much handier on top of that stepladder than I. Let me think a moment. . . . It seems to me that Father used to fold his paper in some way as he put the paste on. Yes, I'm sure he did. . . . I can see him in my mind's eye now, going up the stepladder with the paper folded and letting it unfold, section by section, as he went along. Oh, my! I'd nearly forgotten! When he had a ceiling to do he used to put a plank up on two chairs, so he could walk along it as he spread the paper out. Son, do you have any idea as to where you might get hold of a good stout plank?"

"Yes, ma'am," I told her, "we've got one at the store that I used when I was washing the ceiling. Shall I run and get it before closing time?"

"And you'll have to get another stepladder, too," Grace interrupted. "This ceiling is ten feet high, so chairs wouldn't be any good, or boxes, or anything like that."

"I don't know where I'd find another stepladder," I told her, "but I could bring the ladder I use when I wash the windows. It's not very tall and . . ."

"Never mind the details, but run along and get them quickly,"

Mother told me. "We have no time to waste if we're going to finish papering this kitchen tonight. I'll have the paste ready by the time you're back."

I couldn't hurry very much with the heavy plank and the ladder. When I reached home with them Grace was just starting to paste one end of a long strip of paper, while Mother held the rest of it in her arms. "Good!" Mother said. "I'm glad you got here just when you did. You might run around and draw the paper along on the table as Gracie pastes it."

I drew until I was tight against the wall, but Grace had been able to paste only as far as the middle of the strip. "Now just stop a moment and let me think," Mother told us. "Father never used to get his paper strung out like this. He folded the sheet in some manner, and I'm sure he kept it all right on the table as he pasted. But then, we never had so big a ceiling to cover. Gracie, suppose you help Ralph fold that pasted portion together smoothly. Don't let it touch this dirty floor."

If we'd both had four hands, or if our arms had been six feet long, we might have been able to do what Mother told us. As it was, we made sort of a mess of it. Before we had the paper folded back, we'd dragged it on the floor three or four times, put nearly a dozen wrinkles in it, and had paste clear up to our wrists.

"Don't feel badly," Mother told us. "I'm sure that when it's on the ceiling any soiled spots will sponge right off, and the creases will smooth out easily with a little brushing. Gracie, if you'd just fold that half over loosely a few times, Ralph could hold it in his arms while we paste the other end."

Mother's face looked puzzled as she drew the strip across the table while Grace slapped on the paste. But when she'd reached the far wall she sang out, "Now I remember how it's done! This part has to be folded over so that both ends meet at the middle. In that way the whole outside is left dry, then it is simply folded back and forth accordion-fashion from each end. Gracie, if you'll take one of these corners we'll lift this end high and walk forward until it will meet the part Ralph's holding."

Mother's idea seemed to be a good one, but neither her arms nor Grace's were long enough to reach that high. The loop hit the floor and the two pasted sides stuck together before the ends would come within two feet of meeting.

"Hmmmmmf!" Mother sniffed, as she stood pinching her lips and looking at the sticky place between the two ends. "We'll have to go back and try it again. Ralph, try to hold your end real tightly while we get this unstuck."

I braced my stomach against the table while Grace and Mother pulled and the pasted sides came apart with the sound of a dozen little pigs at a trough.

It took us nearly an hour to get that piece of paper folded so that the two ends met, and so that all the accordion folds on each side were even. But when we had it finished it looked real neat, lying there on the table in twin bundles. Mother wiped her hands on her apron and said, "There! That was a lot of work, but we've learned by it. Well, let's get it up on the ceiling. Ralph, suppose you set up the plank now, and Gracie, we'll put this first strip right along the top of this wall."

As Mother spoke, she pulled a gooey end a few inches out of the bundle and said, "Now, Gracie, if you start with this edge square against the end wall I don't think you'll have a bit of difficulty. I'll put a clean cloth over the broom and help you with it as soon as you have the strip started."

Grace needed at least six hands when she tried to get the end of the strip stuck into the corner of the ceiling. She couldn't lift the limp end up without using both hands, and if she did that she couldn't hold onto the bundle of folds. So she held the bundle against the wall with her chest, then tried to make a quick stab into the corner with the pasted end. It didn't work worth a cent.

Grace made the stab so fast that when she reached the end of the first fold, the whole bundle flipped over between her chest and the wall. It kicked her backwards as if it had been a mule. Mother was standing right below her and caught her, but Grace kept a tight hold on the end of the paper, and, of course, the

pasted side was toward her. Her arms must have kept on going when Mother caught her, because she wrapped that paper around her face and head so tight it looked like a hornet's nest.

"That's enough, dear," Mother told her as they wiped some of the paste out of Grace's hair and eyebrows. "We'll let it go for tonight. Maybe tomorrow we might find a paper hanger who wouldn't charge us too much if we hired him to do the ceilings only. I still think we could manage the walls ourselves, but these big, high ceilings are doubtlessly a little too difficult for us."

Mother didn't seem to be at all provoked about the trouble we'd been having, but Grace was furious. And when Grace was furious nothing but a straight out-and-out order from Mother could stop her. She swiped the paste off her lips with the back of her hand, spit it off the end of her tongue angrily, and snapped, "No, they're not! If it took brains to hang paper on a ceiling there wouldn't be so much of it done, and if other people can do it we can do it!"

"Don't be . . ." And then Mother stopped herself without saying, "impertinent." I guess she felt sort of proud of Grace's spunk, just as I did.

Nobody said a word for three or four minutes, but we all stared up at the corner and tried to figure out how we could get the paper started in it. "Well," Grace said at last, "I know how we can do it. It won't be the way a paper hanger would do it, but I'll bet a cookie it will work. Ralph, you pick up the mess, and we'll put it back together again in a bundle of folds. Then I want you to stand tight in the corner, facing out and holding the bundle as high as you can in your arms. I'll hold the end into the corner, and, Mother, you can reach over our heads and sweep the paper against the ceiling with the broom."

"Hmmmmm, that doesn't sound exactly professional, does it?" Mother said, "though I don't see why it wouldn't work. Let's try it."

I think Grace's idea might have worked if it hadn't been for two or three things: Mother was only a couple of inches over five feet tall and the ceiling was ten feet high, so she had to stand on her tiptoes to reach it with a broom. Then, too, we didn't have the paper folded the right way, and I was standing on the wrong side of Grace. She had to pin me too tight against the wall before she could reach over me and into the corner; then there was no room left for Mother to poke the broom in between us. After she'd nearly swept my nose off, and had pushed the pasted side of the paper into Grace's face, she called up to us, "I have an idea! Gracie, you'll have to stand in the corner, with Ralph on the outside. That will leave the dry side of the paper toward you and give me a chance to get at it with the broom."

When we'd switched around, Grace took the limp end of the strip in her fingers, and was trying to hold it into the corner when Mother sang out, "Now I remember! I can see it as plainly as if it were yesterday! Father didn't hold the paper up to the ceiling with his hands; he used to put a wide brush—like the one Mr. Evans brought us—under the end, then push it tightly into the corner."

"Well then," Grace said, "let's have the brush and we'll try it, but you start sweeping just as soon as I get the end in the corner."

Standing the way I was, Grace had to pull the end of the paper right up past my face, so I couldn't see what either she or Mother was doing. And holding those slippery folds of paper up under my chin was like trying to hold an armful of wet eels. I was having a terrible time with them when Mother called out, "There! There! I thought you'd be able to do it all right, Gracie. Now step back a little, Ralph, so I won't brush the pasted side against your face when I sweep."

I should have had sense enough to have stepped back slowly, but with Mother having to stand on her tiptoes I didn't trust her too much with that broom, and I didn't want to get a faceful of paste, so I stepped quick. For a tenth of a second a stream of paper whizzed past my face like a runaway belt on a machine. Then it came to the end of a fold, jerked the bundle out of my arms, and hauled the whole works down on top of Mother's head. She didn't scold me at all, but Grace gave me fits. She was right in the middle of it when the door opened and Uncle Frank came in.

At first he started to laugh, but when he saw how mad Grace was he stopped, and asked, "Didn't you folks know that it's after ten o'clock?"

Mother wiped some paste off one cheek, where the end of the strip had slapped her, and said, "No, we didn't, but do you know anything about hanging paper on a ceiling?"

"Just enough not to try it," he told her. "Pat Skerry does a good job, and he's reasonable. I'll speak to him in the morning. You folks had better leave things just as they are and come on home now."

Grace was still hopping mad, and blurted out, "No siree! Not if I have to stay here all night! I'm not going anywhere until I've got this one strip up. Ralph, fold that stuff and bring it up here again! And Mother, would you pass me that brush he yanked out of my hands?"

"Yes, but I will not stand for your rudeness!" Mother told her. "We are all anxious to do whatever we can by ourselves, and this has been just as exasperating for the rest of us as for you, but it is no excuse for rudeness. Now I shall let you try just this once more; then we will stop, regardless of the outcome. In the morning I will decide as to whether or not we will try to go on with it by ourselves."

While I was picking up the paper and refolding it Grace told Uncle Frank that she was sorry she'd been rude, but she sounded more as if she were saying it because she had to than because she wanted to. And if she wasn't rude to me after I'd climbed up on the plank with her, she came just as close to it as she dared. As she shot off her last orders she was pulling the end of the paper carefully from the bundle and fitting it evenly over the bristles of the brush. I couldn't see what she did after that, but the paper moved slowly up past my face, there was a slupping sound, and Mother sang out, "That's it, Gracie!

That's almost exactly the way Father used to do it! Now draw the brush toward you a little, till you can see if you have the strip running straight with the side wall. Fine! Fine! Now brush a little more."

Grace must have been so busy that she didn't think about telling me to move back, but I had to. That time I moved real slowly, but, because of the way we had the paper folded, it didn't help much. For every foot Grace brushed up onto the ceiling, another foot of the sticky stuff came oozing out of the bundle and slopped over toward me. I was nearly smothered before I could get Grace to stop brushing.

It was really Mother who stopped her. "There! There! That's enough!" she called. Then, while Uncle Frank was helping me get untangled and down from the plank, she said, "I think you have found the knack of it, Gracie, and that we shall be able to do it without help as soon as we've discovered the proper way to make the folds. But there's no use in trying to go any farther tonight; that strip is pretty well worn out, so pull it down and we'll go and get some rest. Tomorrow is going to be a busy, busy day."

I was up bright and early the next morning, but Mother and Grace were way ahead of me, though they hadn't even started to cook breakfast. They had Aunt Hilda's kitchen table piled high with strips of newspaper, folded in about fifty different ways; some with paste on them and some without. "I think I've got it!" Mother told Grace as I came into the kitchen. She was just finishing a strip that she had folded into a neat little stack, and the folds looked like the uncut pages that are sometimes left in a book.

Grace watched Mother's fingers the way a coyote watches a ground squirrel, and she pounced on the package just as quickly when Mother had finished with it. "Wheee!" she squealed. "That will be as handy as a pocket in a shirt! I'll bet a cookie I could almost put paper up alone with it folded this way. Let's hurry up and get breakfast out of the way so we can go try it."

Mother shook her head as if she were disappointed. "It's not a bit professional," she said, "not a bit the way Father used to do it. I distinctly remember that he always began by folding both ends clear in to the middle."

"What difference does that make if it will work this way?" Grace asked.

"None, I suppose," Mother answered, "but the other way must be better or Father wouldn't have done it. I'm just a little bit dubious about this working as well as you think. . . . But then, we'll never know till we try it, will we? Suppose you set the table while I put the oatmeal on to boil. Ralph, did you brush your teeth this morning? It seems to me you're out here awfully early."

It was just after half-past-seven when Mother and Grace went past the store that morning, and they'd already been to the Maddox house for a stepladder, a couple of boards, and a few dishes. I didn't have a chance to go and see what luck they were having before school time, but when I got there at noon the kitchen ceiling was papered about as well as anyone could have done it, and Grace was strutting like a pouter pigeon. Anyone would have thought she'd done the papering all by herself, but I knew Mother better than that; she'd always give Grace the credit, even when she'd done the lion's share of a job herself.

By the time I'd finished my afternoon deliveries Mother and Grace had most of the paper on the kitchen walls, and it was real pretty; yellow, with little bits of white figures all over it— horses pulling carts, tiny houses, barns, ducks and chickens. I'd just come in and was looking at them when Grace yapped at me, "Don't be wasting your time looking at pictures! There'll be plenty of time for that after this house is cleaned up, and we still have a long way to go before we can live in it. Get a pail of hot water and start washing the ceiling in Mother's bedroom!"

"Gracie!" Mother said sharply, "I'll give any orders that may be necessary." Then she looked down at me and said, "That might be a good place to start, Son. With tomorrow being Saturday, you'll have no time to help us in the evening, and I'd like to get that room ready, so that we may be in our own home for Sunday. We'll be through with this border in a few minutes and you may have both stepladders, but be careful of the one from the store—it's rickety."

That Friday night we worked until after ten o'clock, and only stopped long enough for sandwiches and tea—Mother let both of us have it that night, and from then on—but when we quit we had the kitchen and Mother's bedroom ready to move into. Grace helped me wash the walls in the bedroom while Mother painted the woodwork in the kitchen, then we all pitched into the floors with scalding water, lye, and the stiffest brushes I could find at the store. We used water as fast as the stove could heat it, and every pailful we poured down the sink was about half mud. But when we were through the floors were scrubbed right down to the bare boards, and our fingernails were as brown as chestnuts from the lye.

Saturday morning Mother had Mr. Young move in the kitchen table, the bed that would be hers, chairs, bedclothes, dishes, and anything we had a clean place for. At noon Grace brought the younger children from Uncle Frank's house, and we all had our first meal in our new house together. By supper time the paint in the kitchen was dry enough that Mother could hang the curtains, and the house became our home.

Mother wouldn't let us work on Sunday, even at cleaning the house, but she and Grace were back at it early Monday morning, and I helped them in the evenings. By the end of the week we had the whole first floor scrubbed clean, the parlor and the dining room papered, curtains up at the windows, and the furniture moved in.

By the end of February no one could have guessed that we hadn't been living in that house all our lives—nobody but Mother, and Grace, and I.

10

Sunday in Our New Home

W E'D been living in the house nearly a week before we saw our new landlord. He came to see us Thursday evening, when Grace and Mother were patching plaster in the parlor and I was scraping wet paper off the ceiling. Mother answered the doorbell, showed him in, and said, "Mr. Perkins, these are my two older children, Grace and Ralph. I wonder if you'd excuse me a few minutes; my daughter will need a little help before this plaster dries. Wouldn't you like to look through the other rooms while we're finishing? The younger children are sleeping in the one where the door is closed."

Mr. Perkins was a big, portly man with gray hair, and he acted sort of gruff when he came in. He scowled as he looked around at the naked walls and the heaps of soggy paper on the floor, and only nodded stiffly when Mother introduced us. He didn't say a word when she asked if he'd like to look through the other rooms, but turned and started toward the dining room. We'd finished painting and papering that room Tuesday night, then Mother hung the curtains and had the furniture moved in on Wednesday.

Mr. Perkins went as far as the doorway, stopped and stepped back. I saw him glance over his shoulder toward Mother, sort of as if he expected her to be watching him, then he wiped his feet carefully on a gunny sack I'd put down at the threshold and went on. He was gone four or five minutes, and when he came back he asked pleasantly, "Who did the decorating for you, Mrs. Moody?"

"We did it ourselves," Mother said. "Don't you think my little girl does a rather good job of paper-hanging?"

"Very good! Very good!" he said as if he really meant it, looked over at Grace and asked, "Where'd you learn the trade?"

"On the kitchen ceiling," she told him, "but I didn't do it alone. Mother and I did it together."

"You don't mean to tell me this was your first try?" he asked.

Grace grinned and said, "Well, none of it that's up there now. On the first try we got more of it around our heads than we did on the ceiling."

Mr. Perkins laughed out loud and said, "I did the very same thing on my first and last try at paper-hanging. That must have been all of thirty years ago, and on that same kitchen ceiling." Then he turned to Mother and said, "I'm more than surprised by what I've seen. I was pretty well discouraged on renting to a family with a lot of children, but that's about all a man can get in these big, old houses. How many children do you have?"

"Six," Mother told him.

"Well, that's quite a family! Didn't John Durant tell me you were a widow?"

"My husband died two years ago," Mother told him. "My youngest daughter was born five months after his death."

Mr. Perkins looked back into the dining room, where the top of the walnut table shone like a mirror, and said, "I take it your husband left you pretty comfortably fixed."

"No," Mother said, "I was fortunate enough to buy our furniture at what amounted to a give-away price. My husband had tuberculosis; we will make our own living."

Mr. Perkins frowned the least little bit and said, "That won't be too easy—not for a widow with six small children; not in a town like Medford. What do you plan to do, work out?"

I don't think Mother liked the change that had come into Mr. Perkins' voice. Her own was a bit frosty when she said, "I'm very sorry if Mr. Durant failed to tell you the circumstances before we moved in here. I plan to do fine hand laundry here, and if it had not been for the large room in the basement I should not have taken so filthy a place as this house was."

For a second Mr. Perkins' scowl deepened, then it faded and he said, "It was filthy dirty, at that. I should have got rid of those people years ago, but I didn't want to spend a lot of money fixing the place up for another batch of kids to tear apart."

"My children won't tear your property apart," Mother told him coldly, "and I shall not ask you to spend any money on repairs at this time."

"Now Mrs. Moody, don't understand me wrong," Mr. Perkins said in an apologizing sort of voice. "I can see how you're bringing up your children; I was talking about the kind of kids we most generally get in these big, old houses that are not too far from the brickyard district. Tell me more about this hand-laundry business; it sounds like a good idea."

Before Mr. Perkins left we were real good friends. He told Mother that he'd be glad to pay for all the paper and paint we used in fixing up the house, and that he'd have the set-tubs and gas put into the laundry room if she'd sign a two-year lease. Of course, she said she'd be glad to.

We finished papering and painting the parlor Friday night, Mother had the furniture moved in on Saturday, and when we were leaving church Sunday morning Mr. Vander Mark asked Mother if she'd mind waiting a few minutes. She told us to walk along slowly, and when she caught up to us she was all aglow.

"My, isn't it fortunate we got our parlor finished and moved into yesterday!" she said as she took Elizabeth from Grace's arms. "Mr. Vander Mark is sending two ladies to call on me tomorrow morning, to talk about our doing their finer pieces of laundry, and I would be mortified to death if we didn't have a nice clean parlor to entertain them in. I suspect the purpose of their calling at our house is to assure themselves that their garments will be handled in nice clean surroundings."

"Well," Grace said, "if they're shopping around we ought to get their business; I don't think they'll find many washerwomen with cleaner or nicer parlors than ours."

"*Gracie!* Don't you ever let me hear you say such a thing again!" Mother said in a shocked voice. "Although we shall make our living by laundering for others, we shall *never* look down upon our occupation, nor let it degrade us in any manner whatsoever—either in our own minds or in the minds of the community. I know of no more honorable occupation—or profession, for that matter—for fine laundering is an art if practiced as we shall practice it, with the utmost skill and artistry. And as for serving others for hire, that is the foundation of our whole society, whether we be doctors, lawyers, ministers or laundresses.

"One is respected in a community to the extent, and only to the extent, that he or she respects his own position in life. There are doctors, lawyers, and even clergymen who are a disgrace to humanity, and the disciples of Christ were lowly fishermen. I would not, for all the world, have any one of you children grow up to feel that you were less than equal in every way to any other human being who walks the face of the earth."

Grace was acting kind of smarty when she said "washerwomen," but before Mother had finished she was walking along with her head down. "I'm sorry, Mother," she said. Her voice was husky and catchy in her throat when she went on. "I didn't mean that I was ashamed of our taking in washing. I don't know just what I did mean, but it . . . it makes me boil all over to have rich women from our own church come snooping around to see if we are worthy of it, then passing us out a little work as if it were charity. I don't mind doing washing, or digging ditches, or anything else, but I hate anything that looks or smells like charity."

"It will be entirely up to us as to whether or not it is charity,"

Mother told her. "If we give people one penny's worth less for their dollar than they could get elsewhere, then we will be accepting charity. But if we turn out every single piece as though it were to be exhibited, and charge prices commensurate to the quality of our work, then there will be no woman in our church or elsewhere whom we cannot meet on an equal footing. Don't feel badly about your outburst, Gracie. It has cleared my thinking as nothing else could have done, and through it we have been able to chart the course that we will follow."

Whenever there was something that Mother didn't want to talk about any more she'd change the subject quickly. That time she turned to me and asked, "Son, how much coal have we at home?"

"About a bag and a half," I told her. "It ought to be enough to run us through Monday."

"I doubt it very much," Mother said. "There is the feel and the smell of a coming storm in the air, and we must have a comfortably warm parlor when the ladies come to call. I think we'd better start our furnace as soon as we reach home. Since we've never had one before there may be a few tricks we'll have to learn about adjusting the drafts and dampers, so we mustn't risk waiting till morning and then running into some little difficulty."

"I suppose not," I said, "but if we burn up all our coal today we won't have any to keep the parlor warm when the ladies come tomorrow."

"Yes, I'd thought of that," Mother told me, "but if you're up bright and early you could bring us two more bags before you started work, and I hope that will be the last coal we ever buy by the bagful; it costs twice as much that way as by the ton. Possibly you could get our bin boarded up and lined with paper tomorrow evening, then I'd order a whole ton of coal delivered on Tuesday morning."

"If you'd let me get it fixed up today you could order the ton for the first thing tomorrow morning," I told her.

"No, no, no," Mother said. "We shan't work on Sundays unless it is at something that is absolutely necessary. And certainly not at a task where one would get himself filthy dirty. My, how short the walk home from church has seemed! I didn't realize that we were almost at our own doorstep." Mother stopped for a minute, looked up at the house, and said, "Doesn't it look nice with the ruffled curtains at the windows? If we can just manage to hold on until we get a profitable business started, it will make us the finest home we ever had."

As soon as we were inside the house Mother went straight to the kitchen, lifted the lid from the big iron pot that was simmering on the back of the stove, poked a two-tined fork into the meat, and twisted it a bit. "My!" she said, "this piece of neck isn't quite as tender as I thought it might be! But what matter? A pot roast is always better for long, slow cooking, and this will need another half-hour. In fact, an hour wouldn't hurt it. That will allow ample time for Ralph and me to start the furnace and have the whole house warm when we eat. Let's have dinner in our new dining room, then we'll have the whole afternoon and evening to enjoy our nice parlor.

"Ralph, you might run and change your clothes quickly. Gracie, an hour will give you time to cook the vegetables whole, rather than cut in pieces; they always look so much nicer that way. And, if you like, you might whack up a bread pudding. Muriel, could you set the table for us? This being our first meal in our new dining room, we'll make it a real festive one. Let's use the big linen tablecloth and the dishes with the gold band. Philip, you could peel the potatoes for Gracie, and Hal, you might tell Elizabeth a story if you'd like to. I'll run and change into a wrapper for starting the furnace, but we'll all put on our Sunday things again before we sit down to the table."

When I came back from changing my clothes Mother was pouring kerosene into a lamp at the kitchen table. "Isn't it fortunate that Mrs. Maddox used lamps?" she said. "With no gas jet in our cellar this will come in awfully handy. You trot along and hunt up a few sticks of kindling and some paper; I'll be right down with the lamp."

We'd looked at the furnace by match light when we first came to see the house, but all we had noticed was that it was big and a little old. When Mother brought the lamp, so we could really see it, it looked as if it might have been the one that was on Noah's Ark and stood out in the rain forty days and nights. The doors were rusted yellow, the dampers were broken and hanging in pieces, and the pipe to the chimney sagged like a loose rope.

"Oh, my!" Mother said as she shaded her eyes from the light and walked around the furnace. "Why, it doesn't appear to have been used in years and years. My, I'm glad we didn't wait till morning before starting it up! Did you find some kindling?"

"Yes, ma'am," I said, "but wouldn't it be better if I straightened up this stovepipe a little before we lighted the fire?"

Mother held the lamp high, peered around the furnace and said, "It is a little droopy, isn't it? Yes, I think it would be well to straighten it up so that we'll have a good strong draft from the chimney. That always helps when one is kindling a new fire. And you might look to see that the damper is open. Turn it so that the handle is. . . ."

That's as far as Mother got. I'd already put my shoulder under the sag, and when I lifted on it the whole line of pipe came tumbling down. Soot billowed up so thick I couldn't get my breath, and Mother stepped back so quickly that the lamp chimney was knocked off by one of the heating pipes. Quicker than a wink she blew out the flame, and we were left in the blackest blackness that I was ever in. All we could do was to play blindman's-bluff until we found the door to the laundry room and got out of there.

When we reached the laundry, where it was daylight, Mother looked as if she'd been swimming in ink. Her tongue showed bright pink when she spoke, and I'd never noticed before that her eyes were more blue than gray. "Whewwww!" she whistled as she slammed the door shut behind us, "weren't we fortunate that we put on our old clothes and had no more trouble than we did? Just one flicker of flame can cause flying soot in a closed

room to explode. We'll have to wait a few minutes for it to settle before we can go back in there with a lamp."

Grace had run down the stairs as we groped our way out of the cellar, and came hurrying to wipe Mother's face with a clean towel. "Oh, never mind that," Mother told her, "but you might bring me a lamp chimney. I broke the other one when the furnace pipe fell and startled me. As soon as the soot has settled we must get on with our fire building, so as not to keep dinner waiting when it is ready."

Soot had settled a quarter-inch deep on everything in the cellar by the time we could go back in there. "Well," Mother said, "it's a terrible mess, but it might have been much worse. With all that soot in the pipe we could never have kept a good roaring fire in our furnace, and just imagine what a tragedy it would have been if that pipe had fallen when I had this cellar hung full of nice white garments. So often one forgets his blessings in grieving over his mishaps. I'll set the lamp over here where it will be safe, then we'll rattle that pipe back together so that we may start our fire quickly."

Mother could have found a better word than "rattle" for the way we put the furnace pipe back together. It took us more than an hour. The whole twenty feet of it was so rusted that in places it was no thicker than egg shell, and the ends of nearly every section were bent or broken when they fell. Each piece had to be straightened with a hammer, then wired to the ceiling to keep it in place, and Mother used a whole roll of adhesive tape to patch the holes. When we'd finished she called up to Grace, "We have the pipe all mended, and will have the fire started in a jiffy. If you'd like, you might draw a tub of hot water, so one of us can bathe right away."

Mother stood for a minute looking up at the pipe, then she turned to me and said, "Well, it isn't very pretty, but it ought to do the trick until we can afford a better one. Now if you'd just open that upper door and put in the paper and kindling. We won't put on the coal until the kindling is burning brightly; it might smother the flame."

I took hold of the handle and tried to open the door, but it was rusted in place so tightly that it wouldn't budge. Then, when I gave it a good hard yank, the handle came off in my hand. "Careful! Careful, Son!" Mother cautioned me. "I wouldn't for all the world have Mr. Perkins feel that my children were ruining his property."

"Well, it looks to me as if this old furnace would be pretty hard to ruin," I told her, "but I didn't break it. The handle bolt was almost rusted in two, and it came apart."

When I finally managed to break the rust loose and the door flew open Mother held the lamp in front of the opening and looked in. "Good heavens alive!" she exclaimed. "Why, this furnace is stuffed to the brim with ashes and every sort of rubbish imaginable."

Then she called, "Oh, Gracie! Just set everything back, so it won't cook all to pieces, and you might give the younger children a glass of milk all around. We've run into a little difficulty, and it might be nearly an hour before we have the fire going and are cleaned up."

Way back at the time the Smithers family first moved into the house they must have burned cheap coal in the furnace, then come down to old boards and boxes, and finally to trying to keep the house warm by burning rubbish. We could almost tell when the changes came as we worked our way down through the layers. The pit was filled to the grates with coal ashes and cinders. Most of the first foot above the grates was wood ashes, loaded with bent nails, rusty spikes and old bolts, wedged tight around a solid clinker that must have weighed ten pounds. On top of that the ashes were matted flakes of burned paper, mixed with broken bottles, burned and rusted sardine cans, and all sorts of junk.

It was a long careful job to empty the furnace without cutting our hands all to pieces, and when we'd taken all the ashes and junk out we found that the clinker was stuck fast to the grate and too big to go through the door opening. I'd just crawled inside with the hammer when Grace came down to tell us that it was past six o'clock, and to ask if she shouldn't give the younger children their dinner. From the sound of Mother's voice I knew that she was disappointed. "I suppose you'd better feed them," she told Grace, "but I did want so much that we have our first Sunday dinner all together in our new home—with all the nice furniture, and china, and the cut-glass tumblers."

"Of course we're going to have it all together," Grace answered quickly. "I'll just cut a few thin slices off the pot roast and make them each a sandwich to hold them until you're finished. There's water boiling in the teakettle; wouldn't you like me to bring you down a good strong cup of tea?"

"That sounds grand, but don't bother with it, Gracie," Mother said. "I'm just too dirty to think of putting a cup to my lips. By the way, did you draw the bath water? If you did, you might let it run out and draw a fresh, warm tub. We'll be through here just as soon as Ralph has this big clinker broken and we can light our fire."

The clinker didn't break very easy, and I had a lot of trouble in getting it loose from the grate. They seemed to be welded together, and when I'd finally pried them apart I found that the long center grate was cracked right across the middle. The two halves fell into the ash pit when I freed them. It took me another half-hour to put them back into place and prop them up from the bottom with tin cans.

"There!" Mother said as I crawled out for the last time. "It was a lot of hard work, but it was probably worth it. With a nice clean furnace there is no reason why we can't have a bright fire going here in a few minutes. By the time we've taken our baths and changed our clothing the whole house will be lovely and warm. Now you put the paper in—lots of it. Crumple it all up, and tear it a little bit so the match will catch quickly. That's it! Now put it right in the center of the grate and lay the kindling in around it, tepee fashion. We'll put the coal on as soon as the flame comes up bright and clear."

The flame didn't come up bright and clear. When I leaned

in and held a match under the paper a lazy, smoky flame flickered along the crumpled edges, crawled away toward the middle of the heap as if it were ashamed of itself, and then went out. But the smoke didn't. It rose in billows, and shutting the furnace door didn't do any good. Smoke streamed out of the holes where the draft plate was broke off, and all around the edges of the warped door. "The damper in the funnel!" Mother wheezed at me between coughing spells. "Turn it so the handle is straight with the pipe!"

"It's already turned straight with the pipe," I told her.

By that time my eyes felt as if the fire had caught in them instead of the furnace. We were both gasping for breath, but Mother dropped to her knees and tried to blow into the open doorway to the ash pit. "It's just a matter of draft," she told me between blows and gasps. "Bring a folded paper and fan hard!"

I fanned until my arms ached, but all we got was smoke, and that gradually petered out.

"Whewwww!" Mother whistled when the smoke had let up enough that she could talk again. "Well, we didn't have very good luck, did we? There's something wrong here that's keeping us from getting the proper draft. I suspect it's these open holes in the fire-box door. Do you think we could find something to close them with; something that wouldn't burn off as soon as the fire is started? I'd hardly dare use adhesive tape."

I covered the holes with shutters that I cut out of sardine cans, but they didn't help our next fire much, and the smoke poured out again in clouds. It billowed out of the ash pit doorway, and even seeped out of the cracks between some of the lengths of stove pipe. It was the seeping that saved us. Mother went all around the furnace with the lamp in her hand, looking for any handles that might be draft or dampers, and it was she who noticed that smoke was seeping out of only the first three joints in the pipe.

"I've found it! I've found it!" she called out. There was a grating, squeaking sound, and then the smoke stopped pouring out. "Of all the silly things!" she said. "Now why do you suppose we didn't notice that when we were putting those pieces of funnel together? Some careless person has put the handle of this damper on crossways, and we've been trying to start a fire with the funnel closed off tighter than a drum."

Old and rusty as our furnace was, it took hold in fine shape as soon as Mother had opened the draft. Within two or three minutes the kindling was roaring, and the coal caught as soon as I put it on, but the firebox was so big that twenty-five pounds didn't more than half fill it.

Mother took her bath while I was sweeping up the heaviest part of the ashes I'd spilled. Then, when I went upstairs to get my clean clothes, Grace had every door and window in the house open. She and Muriel were driving smoke out with their aprons, and Philip and Hal were swinging the doors back and forth for fans.

I was awfully dirty, and it probably took me longer to take my bath than it should have, but by the time I'd finished and had my Sunday clothes back on, most of the smoke was out of the house and heat was coming up from the registers.

We'd been going to have pot roast with whole vegetables for our dinner, but it was after nine o'clock before we were all back in our best clothes and down at the table, so it turned out to be a little more stew than roast. As Mother had always done since Father died, she sat looking around the table until everyone was seated and quiet, then she nodded toward me to say the grace. I don't think I ever meant it quite so much as I did when I said it that first Sunday night in our new home.

Even though the roast had turned pretty much to stew, it was awfully good eating, and I can't remember many dinners when we were any happier. Mother laughed and joked about the trouble we'd had with the furnace. Then, after the dishes were finished and Elizabeth put to bed, she read to us for more than an hour.

For some reason Mother didn't read to us from the Bible that night, but from a new book that had been given her for Christmas. The name of the book was *When Knighthood Was In*

Flower, and I liked it better than any book she'd read to us in a long, long time.

Usually Mother stopped reading if any one of the children went to sleep, but that night she read on for more than half an hour after Hal had gone to sleep on my lap. When she reached the end of one chapter, she riffled the leaves ahead with a finger to see how many pages there were in the next one. "I really ought to stop right here," she told us, "but we'll never again have this first Sunday evening together in our new home, and I sort of hate to let go of it. Shall I go on and read another chapter?"

11

The Furnace Expert

THE storm Mother had expected set in while she was reading to us. None of us noticed the howling of the wind until she had finished the chapter and closed the book. Then a window blind slammed shut, and when I went out to fasten it I was powdered from head to foot with snow that was finer than sugar.

"Oh, my!" Mother said as she brushed me off. "With snow as fine as this, we're in for a long, hard storm. We'd better go down and close the drafts and dampers on our furnace, so that we'll have a gentle fire all through the night and a nice warm house in the morning."

When we got down to the cellar we found that our fire was far from gentle. A blast of heat rushed out as we opened the door, there was the smell of overheated metal, and a red glow shone from behind the furnace. "Good heavens!" Mother cried, "it's a wonder we didn't burn the house down over our heads! I should have thought to tell you about closing the ash pit door as soon as the fire had caught in good shape."

Mother hurried to the furnace, pushed the ash pit door closed with her foot, and stepped around to the back. "Gracious sakes alive!" she called out. "Just look at this funnel! Why, it's as red as a berry!"

I got there just in time to see her hand reaching for the handle of the damper. "Don't touch it!" I yelled. "You'll burn your fingers off!"

"Don't you *ever* shout at me!" Mother said quickly, then added, "But maybe it's just as well you did this time. Suppose you find a stick or something to turn it with. That's it! But don't turn it too much. All the adhesive tape has burned off the holes, and I'm afraid coal gas might escape if we checked it too tightly. It's deadly, you know, and could kill us all in our sleep. We'll have to check our fire by opening the upper door and letting a cool draft draw in across the top."

"Well, if we're going to get any cool draft I'll have to open a window," I told her. Then asked, "With all the adhesive tape burned off, how can we be sure that coal gas hasn't already escaped?"

"Smell it," Mother said quickly. She stood for a minute or so, pinching her lips together and sniffing, then she said slowly, "I'm not sure, Son. With a cook stove one smells the gas if she closes the damper too quickly after adding coal, but I'm not sure about a furnace. It seems to me I have read that the fumes from a furnace have no odor, and that one may drowse off to sleep from the effect of them, never to wake again. Open a window, Son! Open them both! Quickly! I can't be sure, and we will run no risks until we can learn more about it."

I couldn't open the windows quickly. They were both nailed tight on the inside and there were storm sashes on the outside. I was just starting to pull the first nail when I heard the clanking of a furnace door and Mother almost shouted, "My stars above! Would you look at this!"

I dropped the hammer and ran to peek over her shoulder, but all I could see was a dull glow at the bottom of the fire box, with a bright red circle of coals around the outside edge. "Why! Why!" Mother said. "We couldn't have been reading for more than an hour, and here's our whole bag of coal all burned to ashes. Why, this furnace could ruin us! Fifteen cents' worth of coal in scarcely an hour! At that rate a single day's supply would cost us . . ."

"Three dollars and sixty cents," I told her.

"Oh, you must be wrong, Son!" she said. "It couldn't be that much!"

"Well, there are twenty-four hours in a day," I told her, "and twenty times fifteen cents is three dollars, and four times fifteen is. . . ."

"Yes. Yes, that's right," Mother said in a dull voice, "and for a month it would be . . . let me see . . ."

"A hundred and eight dollars if it's a thirty-day month," I said, "because three times thirty-five is . . ."

Mother cut me off by shutting the furnace door with a bang and saying, "Why! Why! Preposterous! Well, that's the end of our trying to experiment by ourselves. You'll have to be up bright and early in the morning. We must find someone who is really a furnace expert, then you'll have to bring several bags of coal from the store, and go to Medford Square for new flue pipe. I hate to spend so much money right at this time, but with this storm blowing and the ladies coming tomorrow we can't get along without heat."

"Then I guess I'll have to stay out of school in the forenoon," I told her. I didn't give her any chance to say "No," but hurried right on and asked, "Shall I open the windows now?"

Mother didn't answer me right away, but stood sniffing the hot air for a minute or so, then looked around to where the leaky flue pipe had cooled to a dull reddish-blue. "It seems a shame to waste all the heat in this cellar," she said slowly. "Even without a fire it would seep up through the floors and keep the house comfortable during the night. No! No! I can't risk it! I'll set the lamp right here, so that you can see, and you get these windows open while I air the upstairs room thoroughly. I may be over-squeamish, but only fools rush in where angels fear to tread."

If angels go barefooted, as the pictures in our Sunday School magazine always showed them, I'll bet they'd have feared to tread around our house by the time I got the windows open and went upstairs. The younger children were all in bed, covered with overcoats and all the quilts and blankets we had. Every door and window was wide open, the house was already colder than the North Pole, and the wind was streaking through in a hurricane, but Grace and Mother were flapping aprons, trying to drive every bit of warm air out of the corners.

It was half-past-five when Mother called me the next morning. Her teeth were chattering when she told me, "I'm afraid we may have overdone it a particle when we left the cellar windows open last night. This morning there is no water in the faucets, and I'm terribly afraid some ice may have formed in the pipes. If we let them freeze too hard they will burst, you know, and the expense of repairing them might be staggering."

"Do you want me to start another fire in the furnace?" I asked her.

"Good heavens, no!" she said. "We can't risk filling this house with gas again, and besides, we haven't enough coal. I will need every particle we have for the kitchen stove. I have a wash boiler of water heating, and just as soon as it bubbles we must wrap all the pipes with hot cloths. In the meantime you will have to close and secure those cellar windows."

When I'd finished with the windows Mother and Grace were wringing out sheets that they'd dipped in the boiling water. As they went down the cellar stairs with them Mother called to me, "Get right in here and help us. Dip a couple of those bath towels and bring them right along quickly."

I nearly scalded my hands in trying to wring out the towels, and they were still so hot that I had to keep bouncing them all the way down the cellar, but before I could get them shaken out and wrapped around a pipe they'd be almost cold. Then, too, if I touched the cold pipe with a wet finger it would stick and burn like fire.

After we'd made a dozen trips for more hot cloths Mother said, "There! If that won't do it, we'll just have to wait until we can find out how to get this furnace to burn properly. There's no sense in soiling every inch of cloth we own on these sooty pipes, and I think we've warmed them up enough by now to keep them from bursting. Son, isn't it about time for the store to open? You'd better run along and find out from Mr. Haus- halter as much as you can about furnaces, then hurry right back with two bags of coal. I hate to think of keeping you out of school for a half-day, but it may be necessary. Do you think Mr. Haushalter would mind if you were to go to the Square for a new funnel the first thing, then made up the time you'd lost after we had our fire started?"

Mr. Haushalter was late in opening the store that morning, and before he got there I thought my hands and feet would freeze off. "Why, bless my soul," he shouted when he came around the corner and saw me, "there wa'n't no need of you shinnin' out of a warm bed so early this mornin'. Won't be no- body a-stirrin' out in a storm like this lest they're after the doc- tor, and there won't be no coal orders to deliver till John fetches 'em in."

While he was unlocking the door and starting the fire in the pot-bellied stove I told him about the trouble we'd had with the furnace, and about the ladies coming to talk with Mother, and about the rusted flue pipe and the coal gas. Then I asked him if he could tell me how I ought to set the drafts and damp- ers to get the right kind of fire without wasting coal. He didn't answer until he'd tossed a cupful of kerosene into the stove and got the clean ceiling all smoked up again. Then he leaned his elbows back on the counter and told me, "Well, sir, an old furnace is about the same sort of a critter as a wife, and there ain't no more profit in tryin' to tell a man how to get along with one than with t'other. He has to live with 'em a spell and get used to their critchets and crotchets, and there ain't no two of 'em has the same notions, nor keeps 'em for more'n two-three days hand-runnin'.

"Now you take an old furnace in a house with a big chimbley, one that used to have three-four fireplaces to it. Well, sir, apt as not, when the wind's from the nor'east you got to set your drafts and dampers one particular way. Then come a so'wester, that settin' would be wrong roads about; you got to set 'em different. But you tell your ma she don't need to worry none about coal gas with a red-hot flue pipe and the wind a-blowin' the way it's been endurin' this storm. Bless my soul, with the dampers wide open it's a wonder the draft didn't suck the whole blessed fire, ashes and all, right on up the chimbley."

When Mr. Haushalter was all through telling me about furnaces I didn't know any more about running ours than I'd known before, but I thanked him and asked if it would be all right for me to go for the new flue pipe after I'd taken the coal home. He didn't let me get through telling him I'd make up the time, but said, "Lord love you, boy, don't you worry none about the store till you get your ma squared away to home. John and me'll make out all right, and you'd best to get that furnace a-goin' 'fore them pipes freezes any harder."

When I took the coal home and told mother what Mr. Haushalter had said about running a furnace she shook her head and said, "Now doesn't that sound just like a Yankee storekeeper. I suppose we might as well start finding out about these critchets and crotchets, even if we do have to waste a lot of coal, but I won't risk it with that rusted-out old funnel. You take three dollars out of my purse and run up to the Square for a new one. Tell the man in the hardware store that you want twenty-one feet of eight-inch furnace pipe and two elbows. I know the length is right; Gracie measured it. And, oh yes, while you're up there drop in at the coal yard and ask them to deliver us a ton of furnace coal right away. Tell the man we'll pay for it when it is delivered."

Whenever Mother sent me anywhere she always told me to run, but I couldn't have run to Medford Square that morning any more than I could have flown. I had to lean against the wind all the way, and in some places the snow was drifted more than knee-deep. I'd thought that with the wind behind me, the coming back would be easy enough, but it wasn't. The bundle of flue pipe was bigger than I was, and the wind used it for a sail. I don't think I'd ever have got home with it if I hadn't met Al Richardson just as he was finishing his paper route.

Al was the boy I had a fight with on my first day at school, but I liked him better than any of the other boys, and I guess he liked me. If he hadn't he never would have helped me the way he did that day. The wind was howling so loud we couldn't do much talking, but when we stopped to rest I told Al about the trouble we'd had with the furnace, and about the ladies coming to see Mother. We were just coming into our yard when the fire bells began ringing, and I shouted, "Whew! I pity the poor people who had their house catch fire on a day like this."

"That's no fire," Al shouted back. "Two-two sounded four rounds is No School. As soon as I go tell my mother where I'll be I'll come back and start your fire for you. I'm a furnace expert."

If Al Richardson wasn't a furnace expert, he came pretty near being one, and if it hadn't been for him Mother's laundry business might never have got started. He was back at our house by the time I'd finished my breakfast and changed back into my working clothes. And by nine o'clock we'd taken down the old flue pipe and put up the new one. As soon as Mother had come down and looked it all over to see that we had it tight, we started a fire in the furnace, but it didn't work as well as I'd hoped it would. If we left the ash-pit door and the damper in the funnel open it burned like fury, and didn't smoke at all, but most of the heat went up the chimney or out into the cellar. If we closed the drafts, even part way, the heat would go upstairs, but most of the smoke went right along with it.

I knew Al was doing the very best he could, and I think Mother knew it too. It was nearly half an hour after we started the fire before she came down to the cellar again. She looked real nervous, and her eyes were as red as if she'd been crying, but all she said was, "Is there anything I can do to help you boys? I'm just a little mite afraid that if more smoke comes up the ladies may get here before we have the rooms aired out and warmed."

"I'm sorry about the smoke, Mrs. Moody," Al said, "but the heat chamber above the fire box is so rusted there are holes in it, and if we check the fire the smoke goes up with the heat. If we don't check it a little, the wind is strong enough that it pulls all the heat up the chimney."

Mother pinched her lips together for a minute, then asked, "Isn't there anything we can do to prevent it?"

"Well," Al told her, "we could put in both bags of coal and leave the drafts wide open till the smoke burns off, then send the heat up, but that would waste a lot of coal and be very expensive."

Mother didn't hesitate a second. "Do it!" she said. "This is no time to be parsimonious. And if you can get us some good clean heat up there before the ladies arrive I shall be grateful to you for the rest of my life."

It took nearly two hours and both bags of coal, but the house was aired out and comfortably warm when the ladies came to call, and Al and Mother have been good friends ever since.

He and I had planned to have the coal bin all sealed up and finished by noontime, but we hardly made a start on it. The frozen pipes began to thaw and drip at about the time we heard the ladies ring our doorbell. For a while Grace was able to find us pots and pans enough to catch the drip. But before the ladies left, water was squirting from nearly every joint, and the floor was covered with sooty puddles. Grace and Al and I were trying to mop them up when Mother opened the door from the laundry room.

For a minute or two Mother stood in the doorway, looking around the cellar as if she were taking her last look at a world she had loved. "Well," she said at last, "it appears that we have quite a task before us . . . and quite an expense. I should have had better judgment than to have left those windows open last night . . . but there's no use in crying over spilled milk . . .

or spilled water. Now let me think where we'd better begin. Ralph, I've told the ladies that you'd pick up their laundry this afternoon, and they want it back by Thursday. With this storm blowing it will have to be dried inside, and that will mean plenty of steady, smokeless heat. Al, do you think this old furnace will do it?"

Al opened the furnace door, looked inside, and shook his head. "Not without an awful lot of coal," he told her. "Those two bags are just about gone now. I had to waste half of it before I could burn the smoke off, so it wouldn't go upstairs through these holes in the heat chamber. I could go to the pit for some clay, and patch up the holes when the furnace cools off. If it works you wouldn't have to waste so much fuel."

"Ummm, hmmmm, that might be a good idea," Mother said slowly, "and in the meantime we could see what can be done about these pipes. Ralph, do you think the leaks could be mended with adhesive tape? Of course, it wouldn't last permanently, but it might tide us over until we get this first batch of laundry out of the way."

Mother and I tried to bind up the leaks in the water pipes with tape while Al tried to plug up the holes in the furnace with clay, but neither of them worked. The clay fell out of the holes as soon as it dried, and the water leaked right through and around the adhesive tape.

Mother was looking up at the leaking pipes when Al called from inside the furnace to tell her the clay wouldn't stay in the holes. For a minute or two she just stood there, pinching her lips together, then pushing them out and in, as if she couldn't make up her mind. "Well," she said, "my father used to say that it's a good notion to know when you're licked, and I guess we're licked as repairmen. Whether we can afford it or not, we shall have to call in a plumber and a furnace man. But it doesn't seem to me that we should have to bear the full expense; the furnace was rusted out before we came here, and the water pipes far from new. You boys might take baths while I'm getting a bite of lunch ready. Then, Ralph, you might run over to Mr.

Perkins' house and tell him I'd appreciate it if he'd drop by to talk with me a few minutes."

When Mr. Perkins came he and Mother talked for a little while in the parlor, then she brought him down to the cellar. He didn't say a word when he came in, but walked all around, looking up at the pipes and whistling in kind of a tuneless way. Then he looked inside the furnace and all around it. "See you put up a new funnel," he said.

"Yes," Mother told him. "The old one is right over here. You see it was completely rusted through and filled with soot."

"Ummm, hmmmm. Ummm, hmmmm." Mr. Perkins hummed as he stood looking down at the old pipe. Then he looked up at Mother and said, "Now I'll tell you, Mrs. Moody, I didn't figure on spending much money to fix this place up when I rented it for fifteen dollars a month. To put a new furnace in here would cost me near onto a year and a half's rent, and your lease is only for two. How'd it be with you if I'd have new water pipes put in, and just have the old furnace fixed up so it wouldn't smoke?"

Mother had been looking as sad as I always felt when I had to come home and tell her I'd broken somebody's window, but she chickered right up when Mr. Perkins said that. "Oh, I would never *think* of asking for a new furnace," she said quickly. "This one will be quite all right if it's just fixed so that it doesn't smoke so badly. And as for the water pipes, I'd be more than glad to share the expense; it was I who let them freeze and burst."

Mr. Perkins seemed to be as pleased about Mother's not wanting a new furnace as she was about his offering to put in new water pipes. "Oh, I don't know about that," he said pleasantly, "the frosting probably sprung 'em, but it's mostly at the joints where they were pretty well rusted out; I'll take care of it. How you coming along with your laundry business?"

After Mother had told him that she'd just got her first two customers that morning, and that she'd have to finish their work by Thursday, he said, "Well, well! Then you need things fixed up in a hurry around here, don't you? I'd best get to a phone right away." Before Mother could thank him he started away, then turned back and told me, "There's a shutoff for the water under that heap of rubbish in the far corner. You'd better find it and close it before you're flooded out."

12

Full Speed Ahead

AL AND I had to move more than a ton of rubbish before we found the water shutoff. Then we started fixing one of the coal bins to make it dustproof; boarding the walls up to the ceiling, and lining the inside with thick layers of newspaper. Before we had it half finished Mr. O'Brien, the plumber, came with three men, and the foreman of the furnace shop came with two. They were both sore at Mr. Perkins for making them pull their men off other jobs, and as Mr. O'Brien looked over the old pipes and the place for the set tubs he grumbled, "Of all the bullheaded men ever I seen, old man Perkins takes the cake! There's a week's work here for ten men, and him demandin' I get it done by tomorrow night! If it wasn't for him owning a dozen o' these old traps and paying his bills so prompt I'd tell him to go soak his head. Well, 'tis a pretty penny 'twill be costin' him in overtime, and no tears I'll be sheddin' for him neither."

The men were still grumbling when Mother called me, gave me a slip with two addresses on it, and told me I'd better run right along and pick up the ladies' laundry. It was lucky that Al Richardson went with me, and that we took his sled. We'd

119

expected to pick up both baskets on one trip, but the first lady gave us as big a basketful as the sled would hold. It was heaped high, with a sheet tucked in over the top, and weighed about as much as Al and I could carry. The wind was still blowing snow in a hurricane, the sled stuck in every big drift, and the sheet that covered the basket kept whipping up like a sail. Then one of us had to chase shirts and underwear while the other kept the rest from blowing away.

"Good heavens alive!" Mother said when we brought the basket into the kitchen. "Our blessings do seem to be coming in large batches, don't they? The house running over with plumbers and furnace men, and all this nice business coming in. My, my! I hadn't expected anything like this. Have you brought both ladies work in this one basket?"

"No, ma'am," I told her. "We didn't stop for Mrs. Humphrey's. This one was all we had room for on the sled."

"My, my!" Mother said again. "Why, here it is, quarter of four already! It's time you were at the store and Al on his paper route. Oh, I feel badly about this! I told both ladies we'd pick up their work this afternoon, and I'd hate terribly to go back on my word. Gracie, do you suppose you and I could. . . ."

"No, I don't suppose anything of the kind!" Grace told her. "But there's no reason that Philip and I can't go and get it. He'll have to be our regular delivery boy if Ralph keeps his job at the store, so he might as well get started on it now."

"I know he's large for his age," Mother said, "but ten is awfully young to be out in a storm such as this, and it will grow colder as the afternoon wanes."

"Get your coat, Philip!" was all Grace said, but she didn't even need to say that; he was already bringing it from the closet.

Muriel's age was halfway between Philip's and mine, and though she was a shade taller than I she was as delicate as a fawn. While Grace and Philip were pulling on their overshoes, Muriel stood watching them, with a tear in each eye and her lower lip trembling. Mother noticed it, knelt beside her, and asked, "What's the matter, darling?"

That's all it took to make Muriel's tears spill over. "I want to go too," she cried. "Hal takes care of Elizabeth, and everybody does something to help us make our living but me."

Mother took Muriel in her arms, hugged her up close, and said, "There, there, girlie, don't cry. You see, if things go as we hope they will, Gracie and I will be busy from morning till night, and you will be the housekeeper who makes a home for us all. You know, dear, there is no woman in the world who has a more important task than making a home for those she loves."

When I got to the store I found that more than half of our customers had ordered coal. And I was so busy helping Mr. Durant make the deliveries that I forgot all about Grace and Philip until I met them, way up on Washington Street. It was already after dark, the wind was a lot colder than it had been in daylight, and the snowdrifts had been growing deeper all day. The basket they were trying to take home was even bigger than the one that Al and I took. The sled had tipped over, half of the clothes had spilled out of the basket, and Grace was chasing the pieces that had blown away while Philip held the rest of them down and tried to keep from crying with the cold. That was one time when Grace showed that she was really glad to see me. And she didn't try to boss me a bit. We divided the load between the two sleds, and tied them down with the rope I always carried when I delivered coal through snowdrifts. With Philip walking ahead to tread a path, me next, and Grace behind, we got along pretty well.

Our house sounded like a boiler factory when Grace and I took in the second batch of laundry. I didn't have time to go down to the cellar, because we still had a lot of orders to be delivered from the store. But I could hear pipes clanging together, and the sound of hammering in the furnace came up through the registers as if they'd been megaphones. Mother was busy at the stove, and stopped only long enough to tell me, "We're going to feed the men right here, so they won't have to lose time in going home to supper, and they're going to stay till the furnace is all mended and the pipes replaced in the cellar room. The furnace men have promised to start our fire for us and show us how to control the drafts, but our load of coal hasn't been delivered, so you'll have to bring two bags when you come from work."

It was nearly eight o'clock before we finished work at the store and I took our coal home. When I got there Mother and Grace and Philip were dodging around between plumbers and furnace men, cleaning the cellar. Hal and Elizabeth had gone to bed, and Muriel was keeping my supper hot. She had a big apron tied way up under her armpits, and was bustling around the kitchen as if she were getting ready to feed harvest hands. If I'd eaten all the supper she dished out for me I'd have burst.

It took Philip and me all the rest of the evening just to lug the junk and ashes out of the cellar and pile it in the back yard, while Mother and Grace scrubbed the walls and ceiling. Between ten and eleven the furnace men finished their job and built the fire. It burned in good shape, and no smoke went up through the registers, but an awful lot of heat came out into the cellar.

The old foreman showed me how to set the drafts and dampers, then he stood looking at the furnace and shaking his head. "Lady," he told Mother, "we've did the best we could for you, but you might about as leave try to heat this big house with a hot rock. I calculate this furnace is just about as old as what I be, and in them days they didn't know nothin' about insulation. It'll eat fuel like a cow eats clover if you try to heat them rooms in the attic, and if you keep the ground floor comfortable this cellar's goin' to get hotter'n Tophet. Was I you, I'd get me an ash sifter, and at night I'd bank my fire deep with cinders. There's no profit in leaving a fire burn out, and cinders'll save you a heap of coal." He turned to me and said, "Pick out all the dead ones, Sonnie, so's you don't get clinkers." Then he tipped his cap to Mother and said, "Good luck to you, Lady. I wisht there was more I could do to help you, but there ain't."

By midnight Mr. Kennedy and his men had replaced all the water pipes as far as the laundry room. Philip and I had carried out all the rubbish, and Mother and Grace had the cellar scrubbed spick-and-span. It was after one o'clock before we'd all had baths and gone to bed.

The next morning the storm had let up enough that the snowplows were out clearing the sidewalks before daylight, but the temperature was way down below zero. Mother had me put up lots of clotheslines in the cellar, then bring two more bags of coal as soon as the store opened. The foreman had used a bag and a half when he built the fire the night before, but all that was left was a red lump the size of a quart dipper.

When I came home for lunch our kitchen was dripping with steam, and Mother was washing clothes at a pair of tubs set up on chairs. I'd gone down to watch the plumbers connect our new soapstone tubs when Grace called to me from the cellar, "Don't stand there watching like a ninny! Come help me get these clotheslines tightened up before half this stuff is dragging on the floor!"

Our cellar looked like a sail loft when I went back there. I'd put up ten lines before I went to work, and nearly every one of them was hung solid with sheets and pillow cases and towels. "Fine laundry, hmmmfff!" Grace sniffed. "This stuff ought to have gone to the wet-wash! Mother's breaking her back up there, and at two cents apiece the money we get out of this stuff won't pay for the coal it takes to dry it!"

"Well, the washings weren't all sheets and pillow cases," I told her. "I chased shirts and drawers enough to dress half the people in Medford."

"Hmmff! *Under*shirts and drawers! How are we going to make a living on those—at two cents apiece! And all the stuff we could make any money on so fancy that it'll take forever and ever to do it up! Shirtwaists with so many jabots on 'em they'd make a woman look like a pouter pigeon! And every man's shirt with a stiff bosom and forty-dozen little bits of pleats! They must think Mother's a Chinaman! If there aren't at least four-dozen stiff collars and cuffs in the mess I'll eat it, and Mother doesn't know any more about doing them up than you do. They had a special department for them in the laundry where she worked. Get hold of this line and help me pull it up, or we'll have to wash this stuff all over again!"

Grace was still spluttering when we went up to the kitchen, but Mother stopped her. "Now, Gracie," she said, "we can only make this task harder for ourselves if we let it annoy us. I should have made it clear to the ladies that we could handle only their nicest garments, but I evidently failed to do so. Unless we can accept our own mistakes in good nature we are not yet ready to go into business for ourselves. Muriel, could you make a pot of hot chocolate and some sandwiches, so Gracie and I won't have to stop? You children mustn't be late for school."

The stiff collars and cuffs worried Mother a lot more than the number of sheets and pillowcases in those first two baskets of laundry. When I came home from work that evening our kitchen was hotter than Fourth-of-July, the stove top was covered with flatirons, and Grace and Mother were busy at ironing boards. Muriel had kept my supper hot, and as I ate it I watched them. Grace was ironing and folding sheets, and though she made the edges meet square and even she was watching Mother—and Mother was having trouble.

She spread a half-damp collar out on her ironing board and smoothed it with her fingers until there was hardly a wrinkle in it anywhere. Then she took a fresh iron from the stove, hissed it with a finger moistened at the tip of her tongue, and cautiously slipped it onto one end of the collar. The smooth white linen acted about the way still water does when you toss a pebble into it. Little waves rose at the point of the iron and ran ahead of it as Mother pushed carefully. As soon as they grew to more than tiny ripples she took the iron off, stood it on its heel, and smoothed the cloth again. Then she'd start all over, but as soon as the point of the iron reached the damp cloth the ripples would begin to run.

After Mother had made three or four tries, she turned the

collar around, smoothed it out, and started ironing from the other end. The ripples still ran ahead of the point, and when she reached the part she'd ironed first she left a little pleat between them. "Hmmmm," she hummed as she looked down at it, "there seems to be a little knack about it that I haven't quite caught onto. I wonder how the Chinese laundrymen make them come out so smooth and shiny, with a sharp, straight fold at the top. Hmmmm, I have an idea they must press them very lightly at first, then fold them over while they're partially damp."

Mother tried three or four collars that way, but it didn't work; every time the mark of the collar band showed through the outside. Then she tried ironing some of them out flat and stiff before she made the fold, but that didn't work either. Grace and I had stopped watching her when she finally sang out, "There! There! I knew there must be some trick to it, and I guess I've discovered it." She took the collar she'd just ironed by the buttonhole tabs, stood it up, and drew it into a circle.

The back of the circle sagged inward as if it were tired, and the tips flared out like the eave corners on a Chinese roof. Mother looked at it sort of sorrowfully for a minute and hummed "In the Sweet Bye and Bye." Then she perked up and said, "Well, that's that, but I think I know what the trouble is. If I remember correctly, I've heard a man's stiff-bosomed shirt referred to as a boiled shirt. That must mean that they use boiled starch to stiffen them, and I used cold starch on these. Well! Aren't we fortunate that we started in on these collars instead of those stiff-bosomed shirts with their little pleats? Ralph, if you'll be real careful you might iron a few towels while I'm making the boiled starch. Always test the iron with your finger before you start, so as to be sure it won't scorch. I'd like to make a good big dent in this ironing before the evening is over."

By midnight I'd finished the towels, and Grace had done the sheets, pillowcases, and part of the underwear. But all the fancy shirtwaists and ruffled things were yet to be done, and Mother was still working on her first collar. She must have made half a dozen different batches of boiled starch, but none of them worked right. Her last try was the best, but it wasn't very good. The collar ironed smooth, and it stood up all right, but it didn't have any shine to it. I'd just finished the last towel when Mother held the dull-looking collar up in her fingers, shook her head, and said, "It's beyond me! I'd give a cookie to know how the Chinamen do them to make them come out so smooth and glossy."

"Would you give five dollars?" Grace asked quickly.

"Gladly!" Mother answered. "The success of our whole business might rest on our ability to do these in a professional manner." She stood for a minute or two, studying the collar as she pinched her lip with a thumb and finger. "Hmmmm," she hummed slowly, "I wonder if it would be honest for us to send this first batch up to Sam Lee in the morning. If I spend any more time in experimenting we'll never be able to finish the fancy work by Thursday. Now you children run right along to bed; it's past midnight already."

"And I suppose you don't need any rest?" Grace asked.

"I shall have plenty of time to rest after Thursday," Mother told her. "Now you children run along."

Grace could be as stubborn as a donkey, and sometimes she even tried it with Mother. Instead of putting her iron back on the stove she reached into the basket for another piece of underwear, and said, "I'll go to bed when you go."

"Gracie!" Mother said. She didn't say it loud, but there was a tone about it that didn't allow for any arguing.

Grace and I went to bed as soon as I'd banked the furnace for the night, but I don't think Mother went until three or four o'clock. Next morning there were five or six shirtwaists ironed as neat as a pin and laid out on the dining-room table.

13

Tricks of the Trade

SAM LEE'S laundry was squeezed in between the D & H Grocery and Uebel's drug store. Sam could speak only a few words of English, but we'd been good friends ever since I went to work at the store, and we always waved to each other when I passed his window. Wednesday noon when I was on my way home from school I looked in to wave at Sam, and for a second or two I thought I must be going out of my head. Grace was standing behind his counter ironing a collar, and Sam was standing beside her, jabbering and making hand signs. They were so busy that neither of them saw me until I'd watched them for several minutes, and it didn't seem to me that Grace needed very much jabbering. She was going at the job as if she'd done it all her life.

The iron Grace was using was about three times the size of the ones we had at home. And resting on its top there was a long pole, fastened to the ceiling by an oval spring that pushed down on it. On the counter beside her there was a copper can that looked like a pint-sized perfume squirter without a bulb. As I watched Grace picked up a wet collar, snapped it out straight with both hands, and stretched it flat on the ironing

board. Then, with one hand pushing up on the pole, she lifted
the heavy iron onto the middle of it, and rubbed briskly back
and forth until the linen shone like polished steel. As quick as
a wink she swung the iron back onto a resting shelf, picked up
the copper can, put her lips to the tube, and blew a narrow line
of mist along the edge of the collar band. With a flip of her
fingers she folded the collar along the softened line, swung the
iron back, and slowly ran its point along the fold. As the hot iron
moved along it, the finished collar rolled up behind in a perfect
circle, and it hadn't taken Grace more than three minutes to
do the whole job.

Sam and Grace saw me when she picked up the finished collar and stood it on a shelf beside a long row of others. They
both motioned for me to come in, and I don't know which of
us was the proudest, even though Grace tried not to show it. I
wanted to climb right over the counter and hug her, and Sam
bowed toward her two or three times as he grinned and chirped,
"Plitty good, plitty good. Missie plitty good."

"Hmmff," Grace sniffed, "there's not much to it if you have
the right kind of things to work with and somebody shows you
every move to make. Sam's going to give me some of his starch,
and he's written down the place where we can get more of it,
along with the rest of the things we'll need. Now keep quiet
till I get this last collar done, and you can help me take them
home."

As soon as Grace and I were on our way home I said, "I knew
Sam was a good Chinaman, but I didn't think he'd give his
secrets away like that."

Grace sniffed, and asked, "Who says he gave 'em away?"

"You said yourself that he showed you every move to make,
and that he wrote down what kind of starch to use," I told her.
"If that isn't giving away secrets I don't know what is!"

"Nobody gives away the secrets of their business," she said.
"I bought 'em. For five dollars."

"Whewwww!" I whistled. "Five dollars! That's as much as
he gets for doing up two hundred and fifty collars. Why did you

give him that much? It's more than we'll get for all the collars and cuffs in a dozen baskets of laundry."

"Because it was worth it," she said. "And because he's too smart a man to sell anything for less than it's worth. Don't ask so many questions, and hurry along! You've got to go up to the Square before school time and find out why they haven't delivered our load of coal. If we have to keep on buying it by the bag, the cost will make this five dollars look like chicken feed."

When we got home and Grace showed Mother the collars I didn't know for a minute whether she was going to laugh or cry. "Oh, Daughter!" she said in a husky voice as she held one of them up and looked at it. "You don't mean to tell me that you did this all by yourself! Beautiful! Beautiful! Do you think we'll be able to manage the stiff-bosomed shirts?"

"Sure we can," Grace told her. "About half the trick is in getting a lot of pressure on the iron, and even with our light ones we can do it all right if we set a board low enough that we can bear down good and hard."

Mother puckered her lips as if she were going to whistle, and blew out a long, slow breath. "Oh, Gracie dear," she said, "this takes a tremendous load off my shoulders. I was so worried! We couldn't possibly have sent the collars and cuffs and shirts back washed but not ironed. And it made me feel like a criminal even to think of sending them out to a Chinese laundry and then pretending we had done them ourselves. You know, Chinese laundrymen use a strong bleach that rots linen quickly and makes collars crack at the fold. That's why these were sent to us."

"Sure. I know it," Grace said. "That's why we're going to charge five cents apiece for collars and cuffs."

"Oh no, dear! Possibly three, but not five!" Mother said as if she were shocked by any such idea. "I don't believe that any of the Chinese laundries charge more than two."

"Well, even if we did learn how from a Chinese, we're not running a Chinese laundry," Grace told her. "And how many times could they send a collar to Sam before it would crack?"

"I know, I know," Mother said as she held the shiny band

of linen up to the window and watched the light glint off it. For a moment she pinched her lips together, then said slowly, "Gracie, are you sure that Sam Lee didn't have you use some special sort of starch for these? They don't have that glaring, glassy look that one usually sees on work from a Chinese laundry."

"I don't know," Grace told her. "I only know that he took it out of a can on the top shelf, instead of out of the barrel, and he strained it through a piece of silk."

"Hmmmmm. Hmmmmm," Mother hummed. "I think that five dollars was an excellent investment. Let's not make up our minds right now, but five cents might not be too outrageous a price to charge for work such as this."

I didn't have any more chance to see what was going on at our house until after eight o'clock that night. When I went

to find out about our coal the man at the yard said that, because of the storm, we might not get it before the week was out. Lots of other people must have been waiting for coal deliveries, too. That afternoon we had orders at the store for twenty-three bags.

I thought my back would break before we'd finished the last delivery, but it was worth it; Mr. Durant said I'd earned an extra fifty cents, and my pay would be two dollars for that week.

When I got home that night our house looked as if the Ladies' Sewing Circle were having a fair in it. There was hardly a chair or table in the whole house that didn't have petticoats or corset covers or blouses or shirtwaists laid out on it, and Grace even had the piano covered with carefully folded stiff-bosomed shirts. She and Mother were so busy that they barely looked up from their ironing boards when I came in, and the kitchen table was piled with more fancy things yet to be done. When Muriel started to put my plate and napkin ring on one corner of the table Grace snapped, "No, he can't eat there; let him eat in the pantry! He'd be sure to slobber, and we haven't any time to wash and starch that stuff all over again."

I started to tell Grace that I didn't slobber any more than she did, but Mother straightened up from her board and said, "I know how exasperated you are, Gracie, but we are not going to have this bickering in our home."

I've seen Grace take some wicked tumbles off horses, and one time she had the calf of her leg ripped open on a barbed-wire fence, but she never cried when she got hurt that way; it was only when she had her feelings hurt, or when she was so mad she couldn't help boiling over. That night it might have been a combination of both. She swiped tears out of her eyes with the back of one hand, crumpled up the corset cover she'd been working on, and threw it back into the basket. "That's the third time I've done this cussed thing over," she half cried, "and every time I mess it up when I get to that insertion in the yoke. What in the world do women have to have all this lace and Hamburg embroidery and beading and frills and ruffles and fiddle-de-dee on their clothes for? Just to show how rich their husbands are and to make it hard to do up?"

"I know just how you feel, dear," Mother told her. "I went through the same thing when I was learning at the laundry, but as you get more accustomed to it you'll like the frills and furbelows. And just think how fortunate it is for us that the ladies like them too. If their clothes were of the ordinary variety, almost any sort of a washerwoman could do their work for them, and there'd be no reason for them to send it to us."

As Mother talked she went around to Grace's basket, picked up the crumpled corset cover, and spread the yoke out on the board. Then she reached for her iron and ran the point smoothly along an edge of one of the half-dozen strips of inserted lace. "You see, Gracie," she said, "it has to be done with the very tip, and just along each edge, so. Hmmmmm, I don't think this piece will have to be done over at all. Let's see if we can't sprinkle it a bit and straighten it right out."

I wanted to help with the work, but there were no more towels or stockings to be done, and Mother said that Muriel and I should go to bed and get our rest. We went as soon as I'd tended the furnace, but if Grace and Mother went at all they didn't sleep very long. They were both at their ironing boards when I came downstairs next morning, and there were still enough pieces on the kitchen table that Muriel had to give me my breakfast in the pantry. When I left for the store Mother told me to hurry right home at noon, that I'd have to go to Medford Square and find some sort of boxes for packing the laundry. I had better luck than Mother expected me to. Mr. Felton, at the men's shop, gave me thirty brand-new suit boxes. One corner was a bit water-stained, but they were just as good for our use as any others. He didn't charge me a penny, and told me to come back if we needed more.

Grace lined the boxes with tissue paper and laid in shirtwaists and guimpes and jabots, while Mother checked them off on the lists and put a price after each one. And before putting down some of the prices she'd stop to bite the end of the pencil for a minute. "Let me look at that jabot again before you close the box, Gracie," she'd say. "My! There must be eight or ten ruffles to it . . . and all that lace! Hmmmmm. Hmmmmm. There was an awful lot of work went into it, but it's just a jabot. Do you think we'd be justified in charging fifteen cents for it, or do you think it would be better to call it a dime?"

"Fifteen cents!" Grace would say, and put the cover on the box before Mother could change her mind. I don't know why Mother kept asking her questions like that, because Grace always picked the highest price.

I went and borrowed Al Richardson's sled for the deliveries, then had to wait for Mother to write notes to the ladies. I think that writing the notes was an even harder job for her than doing the washing and ironing. Both of them were long, and she had to start over two or three times before she had them just the way she wanted them.

Even then, Mother wasn't too sure. "My!" she said as she read the first note over, "I hope I've been neither too blunt nor too apologetic, but we just couldn't afford to continue doing up sheets and towels and pillowcases at laundry prices. But even with those rates for the flat pieces, these bills seem unreasonably high. Gracie, are you positive you added these columns correctly? Four dollars and eighteen cents seems an outrageous amount to charge anyone for a single week's laundry."

Grace could figure quicker than lightning in her head, and she could think up arguments faster than anybody I ever knew. "Hmmff," she sniffed, "both bills together come to only eight dollars and nine cents, and they cost us two-forty for coal, three quarters for the gas meter, and a dollar for soap, starch, bluing and tissue paper, to say nothing of the five dollars we paid Sam Lee. That's four dollars and fifteen cents all together, and leaves us $3.94 for our labor. Between us we've put in more than eighty hours on the two batches, and that's less than five cents an hour for our time. Do you think that's too much to ask?"

"Well, putting it that way, no," Mother said, "but we were

slowed up somewhat by having the plumbers here—and I wasted nearly a whole evening experimenting on the collars. I'd hate like everything to injure our prospects by starting off with our prices too high."

"And wouldn't we injure both our prospects and our self-respects if we started off with them too low?" Grace asked. "Don't I remember your saying that . . ."

"You're right! You're right, Daughter," Mother said quickly. Then she folded the note over, with the bill inside, passed it to me, and said, "Just give this to Mrs. Humphrey when you take the boxes to her kitchen door, and don't wait for the money unless she tells you to; sometimes people in their circumstances prefer to mail a check rather than to pay their bills in cash. Now run right along, and do be careful not to spill anything off the sled. If you should have an accident, bring the boxes straight back; I don't want that we ever deliver a garment that isn't in perfect condition."

Mother didn't need to have worried so much about her prices; they didn't frighten either of the ladies a bit. Mrs. Humphrey asked me to come in and gave me a handful of cookies to eat while she read Mother's note and looked the things over. When she'd finished, she went into the front part of the house, brought back her handbag, and took out a five-dollar-bill. When I saw what it was I said, "I'm sorry but I didn't bring any change with me; you could have your husband send a check if you'd like to. Mother said . . ."

She didn't let me finish, but passed the bill out to me and said, "You take this to your mother and tell her I'm very much pleased with her work. I didn't expect her to do flat work at laundry prices. You tell her I'll talk to her more about it when we see each other at church." Then she gave me some more cookies, and I ran all the way home with the five-dollar-bill.

Mrs. Sterling was nice to me too, but she didn't give me any cookies. And when she'd read Mother's note she just said that she should have known better than to send the flat pieces, and that all the work looked very nice. Then she gave me four dollars, and told me I shouldn't bother about bringing back the nine cents change, but that I could pick up her basket again on Monday.

Grace tried to act as if she weren't especially happy about the ladies saying they liked our work, but Mother didn't try to cover it up a bit. As tired as she was, she threw her arms around Grace's shoulders and waltzed her around and round the kitchen floor. Then she gave me a quarter and told me to run up to the baker's shop and get a dozen cream puffs; that we were going to have a celebration whether we could afford it or not.

14

What an Ambitious Boy

OUR first batch of laundry was barely delivered before Mother began worrying about the next. While we were finishing our cream puffs and hot chocolate she said, "Wasn't this a lovely celebration! Now let's talk about the things that will have to be done before we start another batch of laundry. First, we must move all our work below stairs, and we must all sit down to meals together; otherwise our home life would be ruined. The laundry room was dirty enough when we came here, but now that the plumbers are through it is filthy. It must be thoroughly scrubbed and painted. Then we must have several wide shelves for laying out our finished work, and a long table for sorting and sprinkling. Could you build them, Ralph, if we were to buy some new boards at the lumber yard?"

"Sure I could," I told her, "but I'd need two-by-fours and nails and spikes, and a saw and a decent hammer."

I think Uncle Frank has tools that he'd let you use," Mother said. Then she turned to Grace and asked, "What do you think, Daughter; if we had a little gas plate down there for heating our irons, could we make out with those we have until we're sure we'll have more stiff shirts and collars to do up? We have

136

so little money left that I'm rather fearful of spending much until our business is more firmly established."

"Well," Grace said, "I think we need irons like Sam Lee's more than we need shelves and a table. For the next few weeks we could lay the finished pieces out the way we did this time, but without good irons . . ."

"No, Gracie! No!" Mother said. "I will not have our home so cluttered up that we can't sit down in the evenings and enjoy it. You are perfectly right about the irons, but we shall have the shelves and table too. Ralph, will you stop in to see Sam Lee on your way to work, and find out from him where we can buy irons and starch such as his? Unfortunately, the note he gave Gracie is in Chinese. Then tonight you can figure out what materials you will need for the table and shelves. In the morning I'll send Philip up to the Square with a note to the lumberman."

Before I went to the store I took Sam's note back and asked him to tell me where we could buy the irons and starch. He seemed to understand what I was asking him, pointed at his pole-iron, and told me, "Go far low, far low! No givee big plice! See dollah, see dollah!" Then he pointed at the note, smiled, nodded his head and repeated, "Far low, far low!" but that was all I could get out of him.

Mr. Haushalter didn't have much trouble in figuring out what the "far low" meant. "Why, bless your soul," he said, "where else would a Chinaman be sendin' you to buy Chinese stuff but to Chinatown? I calc'late that 'far low' business means you ain't to do your tradin' in them fancy emporiums up there where Washington Street commences to go antigogglin'. He wants you to go fer down into Chinatown; down where all them little stores is packed into the alleys like sardines in a can. You know; down there where . . ."

"No, sir, I don't," I said. "When we came through Boston we didn't go outside of the North Station, so. . . ."

"Well, bless my soul, there ain't nothin' to it," he told me. "Just get off the subway at Essex. The streets is kind of catti-wompus in that neighborhood, but you won't have no trouble if you start off towards the east'ard, keepin' your eye peeled for windas with Chinee writin' on 'em. But be careful of them Chinamen. Give 'em half a chance and they'll skin the hide off'n you; you got to dicker with 'em."

"I guess that's what Sam was trying to tell me," I said. "He pointed at his iron and said, 'three dollars.' "

"Then, was I you, I wouldn't start off with no offer of more'n one-fifty. The Chinee storekeeper, he'll likely as not start off at about four-fifty, then you'll have to dicker back'ards and for'ards till you get to the middle."

"I don't think I'll be doing the dickering," I told him. "I think Mother and Grace will go."

"Gorry! Don't leave 'em to go in there alone!" he said. "A Chinee trader'd skin 'em out of their money quicker'n you could say 'scat.' "

"I guess you don't know Grace very well," I said, "but I'd like to go if I had time. Do Chinese stores keep open on Sundays?"

"In Mass'chusetts? Lord love you, no! Don't no stores 'ceptin' drug stores and the likes stay open on Sundays; it's agin the law."

"Well, maybe I could get Mother to let me stay out of school tomorrow afternoon," I told him, "but I don't think so. If she would, do you think I could make the dicker fast enough to be back out here in time for work?"

Mr. Haushalter laughed and slapped his thighs as if I'd said something real funny. Then he rumpled my hair and asked, "You ain't doin' a little mite o' dickerin' with me, be you? If that's what you're up to you're goin' at it in about the right way, but I'd have to talk to John 'fore I told you to take a Friday afternoon off. Would it be all right if we leave it rest till mornin'?"

"Sure it would," I told him, "but I wasn't trying to dicker. Do you think Philip could take my place if Mr. Durant should say it would be all right for me to take the afternoon off?"

Mr. Haushalter laughed again, and said, "Ain't about to leave go of that string if you can help it, be you? Well, well, well, I calc'late your brother could fill in for you if needs be. 'Pears to be a stout little rascal."

"Yes, sir," I said, "he's real strong, and he's bigger than I am too, and he could do you a real good job."

That time Mr. Haushalter only chuckled, then he told me, "If you hang on like that with a Chinee storekeeper, you ought to do all right, but leave us not put no hens to settin' till I've talked to John in the mornin'."

I ran nearly every step of the way when I was delivering my afternoon orders, then I weighed up and tied twenty bags of coal before closing time, so that Philip wouldn't have too much to do if Mr. Durant said he could take my place.

Grace, Philip, and Mother were downstairs scrubbing the laundry room when I got home from work, but Muriel had the dining-room table set and supper all ready. After we were at the table and I'd said grace, I told Mother about going in to see Sam Lee, and Mr. Haushalter's figuring out what "far low" meant, and his saying that maybe Philip could work in my place if she'd let Grace and me go to Boston to buy the irons. Mother looked up at me and asked, "Did he say *if* I'd let you go?"

She kept right on looking at me steady, so I had to go back and explain things, but I didn't mention what Mr. Haushalter said about a Chinese storekeeper skinning her out of her money if she went to do the trading instead of letting me go.

"Ummm, hmmm," Mother said when I'd finished, "it rather sounds to me as though you had engineered this expedition all by yourself, but I don't know that it's a bad idea. Possibly Gracie could meet you at the carline right after school, but first we'll have to see how we get along with cleaning the laundry room. I might not be able to spare both Gracie and Philip tomorrow afternoon."

For a minute or two Mother sat smiling and looking at the wall behind Hal's chair. At first I thought she was looking at the picture that hung there. Then I realized that she wasn't seeing it at all; she was just looking. Without turning her eyes, she asked, "Isn't Chinatown somewhere near Scollay Square, Ralph?"

"I don't know," I said, "why? Is there something you want Grace and me to get at Scollay Square?"

"No," Mother said, "No, I was just thinking. Uncle Levi lives right near Scollay Square, and if you children should drop around to his room at about getting-home-from-work-time, I'd bet a cookie he'd take you to supper with him. I remember when I was a little girl on Grandfather's farm in Maine, Uncle Levi took me to Lewiston with him, and he bought me supper in a little restaurant. It was the first meal I had ever had in a restaurant, and I shall remember it as long as I live. Gracie, did you ever have supper in a restaurant?"

Tears welled up in Grace's eyes before she could stop them, and her voice was kind of thick when she said, "No, ma'am, but Father bought me a sandwich and an ice-cream soda once when he took me to Denver with him."

"Isn't it lovely to have those little things to remember?" Mother said. "And we have so many of them." Then she looked at Muriel and asked, "Girlie, do you think you could put Elizabeth to bed and wash the dishes while the rest of us get at that laundry room? Hal, you might tell Elizabeth a story before she goes to sleep, if you'd like to. Don't you think she'd like the one about Peter Rabbit?"

If I hadn't already guessed how much Grace wanted to make the trip to Boston, and how much Philip wanted to take my place at the store, I'd certainly have found it out in a hurry when we went to work on that dirty laundry room. Anybody might have thought that Grace was the boss of a road gang, and that Philip and I—and even Mother—were just common laborers.

"Ralph," she told me, "you take that half of the floor over there, and Philip, you take this half! Start in the corners and work back and forth across the room! I'll get at the ceiling, and Mother, you could do the woodwork and the lower part of the walls, so you won't have to get up on a stepladder."

Philip was the only fat one among us. He wasn't really lazy, but he didn't run unless he was being chased, and he didn't often make anybody mad enough to chase him. That night you'd have thought there were forty wildcats after him. For some reason he tried to make scrubbing that floor a race between him and me, and Grace did everything she could to help him win. She'd jump down off her ladder and help him every time he came to a real dirty place, and she made me wash places over when they were already clean. It was no wonder that Philip beat me, but the sweat was dripping off his chin like rain by the time he'd finished.

Mother had never let Philip stay up later than ten o'clock, but that night she didn't say anything about his going to bed, and by half-past twelve we had that laundry room brand-smacking clean. The lye made the floor boards almost snow-white, but turned our fingernails as brown as if we'd been husking butternuts.

"Whewwww," Mother whistled as she gave the last window-pane a final polish, "who would ever have believed that we could do this whole job in a single evening? My! Doesn't that floor sparkle! Do you know, Gracie, that if we had the paint bright and early in the morning we could have this room all finished, except for the shelves and table, by the time school is out in the afternoon?"

Philip had been mopping sweat off his face as Mother talked, but the second she'd finished he shouted, "I'll run up to the Square and get it for you just as soon as the paint store is open. I could be back in plenty of time for school."

"My, what an ambitious boy!" Mother said. "This wouldn't have anything to do with your wanting to take Ralph's place at the store tomorrow, would it?"

"If you work in the store you get to eat candy free," he told her.

"May eat candy," Mother corrected him. Then she smiled and added, "But if it should work out that you take Ralph's place you mustn't eat more than two pieces of candy. Now run right along and take your bath, and don't forget to wash the back of your neck and behind your ears. If you're going to the Square early you must hurry right to bed; it's way after midnight."

While Philip and Mother took their baths Grace helped me figure out the lumber we'd need for the shelves and table, and it was after two o'clock before we were cleaned up and in bed.

15

A Mite o' Dickerin'

EVERYTHING worked out fine Friday morning. Philip went to Medford Square to order the lumber and get the paint, and Mr. Durant said it would be all right for him to work in my place. As soon as school was out in the afternoon Grace met me at the streetcar line, and from the way she acted anyone might have thought she was my mother. She had on her high-heeled shoes, and her Christmas gloves, and she was carrying Mother's handbag over her arm as if she were a grown-up lady.

All the way to Sullivan Square, Grace kept scolding at me because I'd forgotten to shine my shoes. And she wanted to see if my fingernails and ears were clean. I tried to tell her those things didn't make any difference when we were only going to dicker with a Chinaman and buy irons, but she wouldn't let me alone. "Hmmmf!" she sniffed. "That's what you think! Maybe you didn't know that Mother gave me Uncle Levi's address, and if he takes us to a restaurant for supper, I don't want to be ashamed of you."

"Well, you won't have to be," I told her. "If you could see the daub of paint on the top of your own ear you wouldn't worry so much about how I look." That was the only thing that kept

143

her from scolding at me clear to Essex Street. She was so busy peeking at the little mirror inside Mother's handbag and scratching paint off her ear that she didn't have any time to pester me.

Mr. Haushalter was right when he told me the streets in the Chinatown district ran all cattiwompus, and even if we'd had a compass we couldn't have gone straight to the eastward. So we kept turning corners till we found a street where all the stores had Chinese writing on the windows and signs. There was a Chinaman standing in the doorway of nearly every one, hiding his hands inside his sleeves and jabbering at us as we looked in the windows.

We were sure we must be in just about the right place, but we didn't see any store with new irons in the window, so Grace took Sam's note out of the handbag and showed it to a Chinaman who was standing in the doorway of a secondhand store. From the way he'd been jabbering I didn't think he could understand a word of English, but he could certainly read Chinese. As soon as he glanced at Sam's note he opened his door and bowed us in as if we'd been a king and queen. Then he went to the back of his shop, rummaged around for a few minutes, and brought back an old iron with a little crack down one side. He held it out to us, with his thumb over the crack, and said, "Velly good. Four dollar."

Grace shook her head and said, "No, that one's no good; we want a new one."

Instead of taking it back, the Chinaman held it farther out toward us and said, "Sree-nine'y-fi'e."

"No," Grace said, "we don't want it. We want a new one."

The storekeeper looked at her blankly, then said "Sree-nine'y."

"It's no use," Grace said to me. "He hasn't anything but secondhand junk in here; let's go somewhere else."

If that Chinaman couldn't understand every word she said, he certainly knew what she meant. "Jus' a minute, jus' a minute," he said, reached under his counter, and brought up a brand-new iron, just like Sam Lee's. He pushed it across the counter toward us and said, "Six dollar," just as plainly as I could have said it.

For a minute I was sort of stumped. I'd expected him to say, "Four-fifty," and I was all ready to say, "One-fifty," but with him starting at six, I didn't know just where I ought to begin. Grace helped me a little bit by giving the pocket of my coat a twitch. "No! One dollar," I said.

It must have taken at least half an hour for him to get down to four-fifty, and I must have lost track somewhere along the line; I was already up to a dollar sixty-five. Grace twitched my coat pocket again, then walked away from the counter where she could whisper to me. "You're doing all right," she whispered, "but be careful of him from now on. Once he made you go up a dime when he only came down a nickel, and if he does it many more times we'll get stuck. It's all right to go to three twenty-five, but don't you go any higher. We'll try some other place first."

It took us another half hour to do it, but we ended up right on three twenty-five. I'd fallen a little bit behind, so that I was at three twenty-five when the Chinaman reached three forty-five, but when we started to go out he came down the last twenty cents in a single jump. That first dicker was our only hard one, and I think our starting to go out helped a great deal. We didn't have to wrangle more than twenty minutes over the price on the smaller gas irons, and not at all over the price of the spring-pole, the spray can, or the starch. And Grace was positive it was the right kind of starch, because it was in little fine grains, like rice.

I think I might have saved as much as fifty cents on the small irons and other things, but Grace nodded her head before I was nearly through dickering, and you can't do any dickering with a Chinaman after your sister has nodded her head. Until the things were all wrapped up and we'd paid our bill, I couldn't figure out why Grace was in such a hurry to trade. Then she asked the storekeeper if he could tell us the quickest way to get to Scollay Square. The map he drew for us was easy to follow, and by six o'clock we were rapping on the door of Uncle Levi's room.

Just after Grace knocked there was a tinkling sound, and

when Uncle Levi came to the door he was sort of smacking his lips and brushing his mustache with the back of his hand. "Come in! Come in!" he half shouted when he saw who we were. "Gracie, girl, how be you? What in tunket did you fetch along, Ralph; a wagon tongue and anvil? How's Mary Emma?"

Uncle Levi was the only one besides Mother who ever called Grace "Gracie." She'd have skinned anybody else who tried it, but I think she liked to hear Uncle Levi say it. She didn't act a bit prim when he hugged her up tight and kissed her, but giggled like a five-year-old, and at first she didn't give me a chance to get a word in edgewise. As soon as Uncle Levi let her go she told him we were fine, and that Mother was fine, and that it wasn't an anvil I was carrying but gas irons and a push-down pole. Then she began telling him about our going to Chinatown and dickering for the irons, and I think she'd have run on all evening if he hadn't cut in and asked, "Et your victuals yet?"

"No, sir," I said before Grace had any chance to head me off.

But I guess she didn't think that was polite enough, and that she could fix it up so we wouldn't sound too anxious. "Oh, we mustn't stop . . . long," she said, "Mother might worry about us. But, being right in the neighborhood, we thought we'd just stop in for a minute and say hello."

"Thought you said you was down to Chinatown," Uncle Levi said.

"We were," Grace told him. "We just stopped by on our way . . . on our way to the subway."

"Why, child alive," he said, "there's half a dozen subway stations twixt here and Chinatown. Didn't you see. . . ."

When we'd come in I'd set the box of irons down right by the door, and as Uncle Levi was talking he bent over to move it. He'd just lifted it off the floor when he stopped in the middle of what he was saying and asked me, "You didn't lug this cussed anvil all the way from Chinatown, did you?"

Grace started right in to tell him again that it wasn't an anvil, but that time I interrupted her and said, "Yes, sir. It got kind of heavy along toward the last end."

"It's a God's wonder you ain't pulled your arms out," he told me. "By hub, it must weigh nigh onto forty pounds. You children hold on till I go wash my hands, and we'll hunt up some victuals. Want to come along with me, Ralph? Gracie, you'll find the place where ladies wash their hands down tother end of the hall."

I'd bet almost anything that Grace found a big mirror in that ladies' washroom. We had to wait nearly fifteen minutes for her, and when she came back she was all primped up, with little spitcurls peeping out from under her hat. Maybe it was just as well she took so long. It gave me a chance to tell Uncle Levi about our renting the big house on Spring Street, and our fixing it up, and Mother's getting two customers, and about the shelves and table I was going to build for her.

When Grace finally did come back Uncle Levi sang out, "By hub, if you ain't a spittin' image of Mary Emma whenst she was commencin' to grow up, my recollection's playin' tricks on me. Now, m'fine lady, where'd you like to eat your victuals?"

Grace patted her hair a couple of little dabs, and said, "Oh, we really mustn't . . ."

I didn't let her get any further, but said, "I saw a place in Scollay Square where a man in a white uniform was frying biscuits in the window."

"Griddle cakes," Uncle Levi said, "and tolerable good eatin', too, along with a couple o' pork chops and applesauce, and mashed potatoes and pan gravy, and butter beans and squash pie. Them Childs folks whacks up a larrupin' good squash pie. How'd you like that, Gracie?"

If Grace ever had an idea that Mother would be worried about us she forgot it as soon as we sat down at the table in Childs. She didn't usually talk very much, but that night she was wound up tighter than a dollar watch. She told Uncle Levi about Mother's buying a whole houseful of real nice furniture for only fifty dollars, and about Mr. Perkins having the new soapstone tubs put in the laundry room, and everything else she could think of.

I ate so much that it's a wonder I didn't pop, but that was only because I didn't have anything else to do. Grace didn't let me get more than two or three words in until she'd told Uncle Levi about Mother's insisting that all the laundry work be done in the basement, and about our cleaning up the laundry room, and what color she and Mother had painted it that morning, and that there was nothing left to be done except for me to build the shelves and table.

I think she'd have kept right on going if Uncle Levi hadn't looked over at me and asked, "What kind o' nails you goin' to use?"

"Eight pennies, and sixteen-penny spikes," I told him.

"Commons?" he asked.

I didn't know just what he meant, so I said, "Well, just ordinary nails and spikes; I suppose they're common."

"Got 'em bought yet?" Uncle Levi asked me.

Before I could answer him Grace said, "Yes, sir. And the lumber and the ton of coal we've been waiting for, too. The men were just delivering them when I left the house."

"You don't say," Uncle Levi said, sort of as if he were thinking about something else. Then he asked, "Frank's folks been over since you got the place fixed up?"

"Uncle Frank has been over several times," Grace told him, "but Aunt Hilda and the children haven't. Mother says that when we get everything all finished we're going to have a housewarming. Then they'll all come over for a Sunday dinner with us, and we hope you'll be able to come, too."

"By hub, I will. I will," Uncle Levi said quickly. "Always did like a housewarmin'. Like to see all the little shavers roundabout a big table, pokin' away the victuals till they're fit to bust. Always did calc'late that folks ought to move about onct a year, so's to have plenty of housewarmin's."

As Uncle Levi spoke he took his big watch out of his vest pocket, glanced down at it, and said, "By hub, here it is nigh onto eight o'clock. If Mary Emma's goin' to worry about you children she's likely hard at it a'ready. Leave me lug that anvil,

Ralph; I'll see you over to the subway and get you headed in the right direction. For folks that ain't used to it, Boston can be devilish hard to find your way about after nightfall."

Uncle Levi took us as far as the entrance to the subway station, and after we'd thanked him for our supper he told us, "Don't never thank me for victuals! If there is anything in this world I like to see better'n a parcel of little shavers sittin' up to table and stuffin' their bellies, I don't know what it is. You tell Mary Emma I ain't goin' to wait much longer for that house-warmin' of hers."

I was so full of supper that I couldn't help going to sleep on the subway train, so I don't remember much about that trip home, except that our feet nearly froze on the way from the carline to our house, and that the box of irons grew heavier with every step.

Mr. Haushalter told me that Philip did a real good job at the store, and at nine o'clock that Saturday night Mr. Durant called me over to his desk and gave me a two-dollar bill. "I didn't pay your brother," he told me. "You can settle that between you. The extra fifty cents is for those rough evenings we had during the storm." Before I left for home I changed the bill, so I'd have a fifty-cent-piece for Philip.

Hal and Elizabeth had gone to bed before I got home, but the rest of the family was in the parlor, and Mother was reading aloud. I came in through the kitchen door, put my dollar and a half in Mother's purse, and took the fifty-cent-piece in to Philip. He grinned from ear to ear when I gave it to him, and then took it over to Mother. "Isn't that nice?" she said as she looked up from the book. "Why don't you put it in that little bank that came with our furniture and save it?"

"Doesn't Ralph put his money in your purse?" he asked her.

"Why yes," Mother told him, "but, you know, Ralph is the man of our family, and . . ."

Mother must have noticed as quickly as I did that Philip's lip was beginning to tremble, because she hesitated for only a moment before she went on, ". . . and you are my man, too, so you run right out and put your half-dollar in with Ralph's."

I think Philip was as proud of earning that fifty cents as if it had been fifty dollars, and he was all smiles again when he came back to the parlor. Mother read to us that night until after eleven o'clock.

16

Housewarming

OF COURSE I knew that Mother would let us work on Sunday only when it was absolutely necessary, but I was anxious to find out what kind of a job I could do on the shelves and table for the laundry room. So when we were finishing breakfast Sunday morning I said, "I guess I'd better get started on those shelves and the table right away, or else they won't be ready for our next batch of laundry tomorrow."

"Oh no, Son," Mother said, "not on Sunday! Sunday is a day of rest. You'll have plenty of time to nail those boards together tomorrow evening. You children must hurry right along with your baths, so you won't be late for Sunday School. I'm afraid that 'hen' we got at such a bargain has turned out to be a rooster, but it should make us a good stew if it simmers slowly while we're at church. Hal, suppose you take Elizabeth into the parlor and tell her a nice long story while we're clearing up the breakfast dishes."

I'd just finished my bath when Hal came running back from the parlor shouting, "Mother, a two-wheeled buggy has stopped in front of our house, with a man on a little seat way up high in back."

We all went running to peek out the front windows, and, sure enough, there was a hansom cab standing in front of our house. The driver was climbing down from his seat, and Uncle Levi was coming out of the cab, seat first. He was just about wide enough to fill the whole doorway. Mother didn't even stop to take off her apron, but ran onto the piazza, calling, "Uncle Levi! Uncle Levi! Oh, I'm so glad to see you! Why didn't you let us know you were coming, so the boys could have met you at the carline?"

"Wa'n't no sense of that; I didn't come on the streetcar," Uncle Levi called back as Mother ran toward him, "and I told Gracie and Ralph to tell you . . ."

By that time Mother had reached him, and he hugged her up over his stomach until only her toes were touching the snow. "What did you tell the children, you old rascal?" she asked him as soon as he stood her down.

"Told 'em to tell you I wa'n't goin' to wait much longer for you to have a housewarmin', and, by hub, I wa'n't. I fetched it with me. Ralph, come help me lug some of this rubbish into the house. Why, Mary Emma, it's a right nice-lookin' place you got here. How be you, Gracie? And there's Muriel, and Phil and Hal and the baby. Named her Elizabeth after your mother, didn't you, Mary Emma? You get back inside 'fore you catch your death-o-cold; I and the boys'll fetch the stuff in."

Uncle Levi turned back to the hansom cab and began handing out bundles, boxes, jugs and bags as if he were unloading a farm wagon. They came so fast that I could only pile them up on the sidewalk, and it looked as though he'd bought out half the stores in Boston. There were two great big bags of fruit, every sort of vegetable you could think of, a turkey that weighed nearly as much as Elizabeth, a two-gallon jug, and a dozen or so packages that were tied up so that I couldn't see what was in them. After all the packages and bags were out he passed me what I thought was a wooden suitcase, but the minute I got hold of it I knew from the weight that it was a tool box. Then, without turning around, he asked, "Where's Phil?"

"Right here!" Phil called from beside me.

"Ain't you the delivery man?" Uncle Levi asked.

"Yes, sir. Or, anyway, I'm going to be," Philip told him.

"So I heard tell. Calc'lated you might need a sled, so I fetched one along. Snow's no use to a boy lest he's got a sled."

As Uncle Levi talked he backed out of the cab, holding a sled that was nearly as long as he was tall, and had *Flexible Flyer* painted on it in bright red letters. "Kind of long for belly-bump slidin'," he said as he passed it to Philip, "but mebbe it'll do for haulin' wash baskets. How 'bout you skedaddlin' over to Frank's house and tellin' 'em we're havin' a housewarmin'? Tell Frank to fetch his tools along, and his overhauls; we got a job o' work to do."

If that wasn't the first steering sled in Medford, except for double-runners, it came pretty close to being, and it was certainly the best one. Philip would hardly take his hands off it long enough to go into the house for his overcoat and mittens.

As soon as Uncle Levi had paid the cabby I told him to go right into the house, that I'd bring the packages. But I didn't hurry. With every armful I expected Mother to say, "Now hurry right along, Son; you children mustn't be late for Sunday School." She didn't say it, though, and none of us reminded her.

When I carried the last load into the kitchen Mother was sitting on Uncle Levi's lap and laughing as he bounced her up and down and sang, "Round and round the cobbler's bench." I'd saved the turkey back for the last, and as I brought it in Mother cried, "My stars, Uncle Levi! Why you've brought enough to feed an army! What in the world will we ever do with it all?"

"Eat it! Eat it! It's all good victuals!" Uncle Levi sang out. "By hub, ain't we goin' to have fun!" Then he stopped bouncing Mother, and asked, "Did you fetch in my tool case, Ralph?"

"Yes, sir," I told him. "I put it in the laundry room down in the basement."

"Ain't it about time we was gettin' at that table?" he asked me. "The women folks won't want us clutterin' up their kitchen whilst they're cookin' the victuals."

"Oh, Uncle Levi, you know I'd love to have you right here where we could visit," Mother said quickly. But she didn't say anything about Sunday being a day of rest, and she didn't make any fuss when I went up to my room and put on my overalls.

I never thought there'd be a man I'd like to work with as well as I used to like working with Father, but Uncle Levi came awfully close to it. When I took him down to the laundry room he took off his coat and collar, rolled up his shirt sleeves, and pulled on the overalls he'd brought in his tool case. Then he stood looking down at the little pile of lumber for a minute or two, and said, "By hub, it looks like they run it through a coffee mill, 'stead of a planer. Must'a picked over forty-'leven stacks to find it. How was you calc'latin' on buildin' the table?"

"Well," I told him, "I was planning to saw one of these two-by-fours into pieces for the legs, then spike other pieces on one end of them to make a frame, and nail the boards on top. Mother wants the table ten feet long and . . ."

I was still telling him when Uncle Frank called, "Hi there, Levi!" from the top of the stairway.

"Get your overhauls on and fetch your tools down," Uncle Levi called back to him. "We got a job o' work on our hands, and a mess o' lumber that ain't fit for makin' hog-troughs."

"Be with you soon's I get Hilda started off," Uncle Frank called back. "She's going to roast the turkey over home. One stove won't handle all the stuff." Then I heard him say, "Oh, let 'em both go, Mary Emma; that sled will hold a dozen young-sters."

Uncle Levi was still looking over the lumber and sorting it out when Uncle Frank came down to the laundry room. "What did they send her, a bunch of number-two stuff?" he asked as he came in.

"Number two!" Uncle Levi grumbled. "Number nine, ten, 'leven! It's a God's wonder they could get it through a doorway!

Hard pine boards warped till they look like ribbon candy, and brittle as glass. Split like kindlin' if you was to drive a nail into 'em. Hemlock two-by-fours, and there ain't one of 'em but what's twisted like an auger bit. By hub, I'd like to lay hands on the man that'd send this kind o' rubbish to a widda-woman, but it's too late to send it back now. Let's heist some o' these straightest boards atop the tubs here, so's to make a bench."

Father had always been careful with his tools, and about the way he put them into his tool box, but nothing compared to Uncle Levi. Every tool was fastened into its own place, every plane blade and chisel was as sharp as a razor, and down each side of his case he had little drawers for finish nails and brads and screws and flake glue. When all the tools were laid out the way he wanted them, he set a little pot of glue to simmer on the furnace, and told us, "Don't calc'late we can make a silk purse out of a sow's ear, but like as not we can work the worst kinks out'a this stuff. Frank, you could do the rippin' if you've a mind to. And, Ralph, you can look after the planin' whilst I do the markin' out and cut the mortises and tenons. Don't try to take too big a bites; a deep cut would rough up them cussed knots. Slow and easy goes fer in a day."

When we'd finished our jobs we had four of the prettiest table legs you could find. Each one was as straight as a gun barrel, tapered evenly from its two-by-four shoulder to the inch-square end that would sit on the floor, and mortised perfectly on two sides. Uncle Levi picked our straightest boards for side and end stringers. When they had been ripped, planed, and tenoned, I painted the inside of the mortises with hot glue, and the pieces fitted together as perfectly as if they'd been the parts of a fine watch.

It seemed to me that it was a shame to make so fine a table frame when we had only warped boards for the top and under shelf, but the boards weren't warped when Uncle Levi had finished with them. He planed the edges until they fitted with barely a hair line between them, bored holes in the sides, and glued dowel pins tightly into them as Uncle Frank and I sprung out the warp. Then he had us squeeze the boards snugly together while he screwed them into place from underneath, so that no holes showed from above. When the top and under shelf were planed and sandpapered, they were as smooth and even as if they'd been made of glass.

"There!" Uncle Levi said as he stood back and looked at the table. "Calc'late that'll come nigh to fetchin' it, soon's I whack up a couple o' drawers and fit 'em in; a table ain't no good without drawers."

I was still rubbing my hand over the table top when Mother called down from the head of the kitchen stairway, "How would you men like some hot apple pie and doughnuts? That turkey's so big it will take at least six hours to roast, so we won't have dinner till nearly four, but I've just taken a pie out of the oven, and Gracie will have doughnuts out of the kettle in a few minutes."

"By hub, that would hit the spot!" Uncle Levi shouted back. "And how 'bout sendin' down a pitcher o' cider? I'm dryer'n a toad in hayin' time."

I'd expected Mother or Grace to bring the lunch down, but it was Muriel who brought it. She had Mother's best apron on, with the top tied just below her armpits and the hem nearly touching the floor, and she was as businesslike as if she'd been a regular waitress in a restaurant. "Calc'lated you little shavers would all be out slidin'," Uncle Levi said when she came in.

"They are," Muriel told him. "Philip has slid John and Hal and Elizabeth all over town to show off his new sled, but, you know, I'm the housekeeper; I have to stay here to take care of things while Mother and Grace are cooking. And I'm minding Louise while Aunt Hilda's over at her house roasting the turkey. Oh my! I forgot to bring a tablecloth, and we mustn't get any spots on that pretty table before Mother sees it."

She'd brought a whole apple pie on a big tray, and plates and forks and glasses, but no knife to cut the pie with. While she was gone for the tablecloth Uncle Levi kept looking at the pie and smacking his lips. "By hub," he said, "I wisht the little tyke would forget 'bout that tablecloth, and fetch a knife and a pitcher o' cider. Don't know where a man could find better victuals than fresh apple pie, lest it's hot doughnuts with a dollop o' sweet-apple cider to wash 'em down."

We ate the whole pie, and about two-dozen red-hot dough-nuts—just as fast as Grace could fish them out of the kettle—and drank the whole pitcher of cider. "By hub, it's a God's wonder I ain't busted a seam," Uncle Levi said as he got up from the table. "Whilst I'm whackin' together a couple o' drawers you boys might get to goin' on them shelves Mary Emma wants for layin' out her fancy work. We ought to have just about time to finish up 'fore the turkey's roasted and the main victuals is ready."

"I don't think we'll be able to do much about the shelves," I told him. "I didn't plan on an underneath shelf, or drawers, or board stringers for the table when I made out the order for the lumber, so we're six boards short and two two-by-fours over."

"So much to the good!" Uncle Levi told me. "You wouldn'ta been able to do no good with them rock-hard, warped boards no way, and you can rip the two-by-fours in half for uprights; that'll give Mary Emma stouter shelves; ones that won't sag whenst she puts a load on 'em."

He turned to Uncle Frank and told him, "Frame it up, same's you would for a cupboard, and make it two boards deep, so's she'll have plenty of room; you could rip crossbars out'n some of this waste. Notch them two left-over boards for the bottom shelf, but don't nail 'em down. That way Ralph can use 'em for a pattern when he goes to cut the balance. And, Ralph, you tell that lumberman to send you number-one-clear white pine boards that's milled smooth, or I'll be up there to settle with him."

"And if he soaks you over four cents a board foot," Uncle Frank told me, "you can tell him I'll be up there to find out the reason for it."

Uncle Frank and I had finished the frame for the laundry

shelves, and Uncle Levi was just slipping the second drawer into the table when Mother called from the top of the kitchen stairs, "Twenty minutes, and everything will be on the table! You carpenters had better knock off and get washed up."

When we had finished the pie and doughnuts I was so full that I thought I'd never want to eat again, but the smells that came down the stairway when Mother called us brought my appetite back in a hurry, and I felt as if I were starving to death.

I'd barely scrubbed my face and hands and changed back into my Sunday clothes when Philip pulled his sled up to our back steps and shouted, "Ralph, come help me with this turkey; it weighs a ton!"

Aunt Hilda had put the turkey—roasting pan, gravy and all—into her copper wash boiler, and wrapped it up in a heavy quilt to keep everything hot. Hal and John were sitting on the sled, facing each other and holding the boiler between their legs, and Aunt Hilda was carrying Elizabeth. She seemed to be a little bit nervous when Philip and I were carrying the boiler up the slippery steps, but she didn't say anything, and we were so careful that we didn't even slop a drop of gravy out of the pan.

We've had some pretty good dinners at our house, but never one that was any better than the dinner we had that day. And nobody could have guessed it was a housewarming instead of Thanksgiving. I'd expected that Mother would put Uncle Levi at the head of the table, but she didn't. When everything was ready, she put Elizabeth in the highchair beside her place, looked down the long table, and said, "Now let's see where we will put everybody. John, would you like to sit at the first place on this side, and then Hilda, and Frank, and Philip. And girls, I'm going to let you share Uncle Levi between you, so, Hal, you sit here by me." That left only Father's place for me, with the turkey right in front of it.

I don't think I did a very good job of asking the blessing, because I was too much worried for fear I'd mess up the turkey in trying to carve it. But I guess Mother knew I was worried. As soon as we'd raised our heads, she said, "Frank, I wonder if you'd carve the turkey for us? That would let Ralph serve it while it's piping hot, and I'll put the vegetables and gravy on the plates."

Uncle Frank was an expert carver, and he seemed to know right where all the joints were. It didn't take him more than a minute to clip off the drumsticks and thighs, then he peeled off thin slices of white meat that were as big as his hand. I knew enough to serve Aunt Hilda first, and that ladies usually liked the white meat best, so I put a spoonful of stuffing at one side of her plate, and laid two of the biggest slices over it. "That's for Aunt Hilda," I said, as I put on the cranberry sauce and passed the plate along for Mother to put on the mashed potatoes, and sweet potatoes, and boiled onions, and carrots, and turnips and gravy.

I'd just laid a thigh on the next plate, and was reaching for a spoonful of stuffing when Uncle Frank cut off the turkey's tail and whispered to me, "If that's for Levi, set Old John Barley-corn's nose right atop the stuffing, and smear a little cranberry juice on it."

Everybody had been quiet, and sort of on their manners, until I passed the plate down the table and said, "That's for Uncle Levi." Then the fun began, and it lasted until we were all so stuffed we didn't have room for any fruit or pumpkin pie. I can't remember ever having seen Mother laugh and enjoy herself so much.

"There, by hub!" Uncle Levi said as he pushed his chair back. "That's what I call a housewarmin'! As I was tellin' Gracie, I calc'late a family ought to move about onct a year, so's to get in plenty o' housewarmin's whilst the children is all together."

Mother's face grew sober as if she were sad, and she said, "It was a lovely housewarming, but I hope we don't have to move again for a good many years. I only pray that we may be successful enough with our little business that we can stay right here."

"Ain't no doubt of it!" Uncle Levi said quickly. "Ain't no doubt of it! Father was an old man whenst I was born, and he wa'n't overly religious, but I recollect his tellin' me, 'Pray to God to help you, then work just as hard as if you hadn'ta prayed.' The way you folks has been workin', I don't calc'late the Almighty's about to let you down."

As Uncle Levi spoke, he'd been fumbling at his vest pocket for his watch. After he'd finished, he pulled it out, glanced at it, and shouted, "Jumpin' Jehoshaphat! It's nigh onto seven o'clock! Who'd a'thought we'd been sittin' here to table for three hours! By hub, sit here much longer'n I'll be ready to start all over again! Phil, take a look and see if that cabby's waitin' for me out front. Told him to pick me up at seven sharp; that cussed tool case o' mine's too heavy to lug on the streetcars."

17

Another Mark Against Me

MOTHER was as anxious to have me finish building the shelves in the laundry room as I was to do it. While we were eating breakfast Monday morning, she asked, "Ralph, do you think Philip's sled would be sturdy enough to carry as many boards as you'll need to finish out those shelves for us?"

"Sure it would," I told her. "We only need ten boards, and if they're white pine they won't weigh over a hundred pounds, and that sled is stout enough to carry nearly half a ton."

"I'll betcha it would carry a whole ton!" Philip sang out. "I could get the boards for you, Mother. If I start right after breakfast I could be back in plenty of time for school."

Mother smiled and said, "I'm afraid that's a little too big a job for a ten-year-old. But if you boys were to hurry right home from school this noon I could have lunch all on the table, and a note ready for the lumberman. Ralph, do you think that would give you time enough that you positively wouldn't be late for school?"

"I guess so," I told her, "but if you had sandwiches ready, so we could eat them on the way, I'd be positive."

"Very well," Mother said. "I'm anxious to have those shelves all ready by the time we start our ironing, and with all this snow on the ground I doubt that the lumberman would send out a special wagon with so small a delivery. Then, too, that would leave Philip with his sled free for picking up the ladies' baskets after school."

If we had still been in Colorado I could have been out of school within half a minute after the twelve o'clock bell rang, but it didn't work that way in Medford. We had monitors that brought our coats and caps and rubbers from the coatroom when the bell rang. And after we had them on we had to form lines outside our classrooms, marking time like soldiers, while a teacher played the piano in the downstairs hall and Mr. Jackman went all around the building to inspect us. I don't think he liked me very well since I hit him by mistake when we first moved to Medford, and he always seemed to inspect me the hardest.

That day I was thinking about wanting to get out in a hurry, and about what I was going to say to the lumberman, and I sort of forgot about marking time until I heard Mr. Jackman call out, "Feet high, children! One, two, three, four; one, two, three, four," as he came down our line toward me. He was almost to me before I noticed that I wasn't lifting my feet, and I didn't want to give him any excuse for scolding me, so I started lifting them in a hurry, but I started a little bit too hard. My knee bumped the girl in front of me when Mr. Jackman was right beside her.

She squealed and jumped about a foot high, and Mr. Jackman pounced on me like a coyote on a prairie dog. He jerked me out of line and shook me till my teeth rattled like stones in a tin can. Then he told me that he wouldn't tolerate any smart aleck boy getting fresh with the girls in Franklin School, and that if he ever caught me at it again he'd expel me altogether. He wouldn't believe me when I told him that I didn't do it on purpose, and made me stand marking time until the very last line had marched out of the schoolhouse. Before he let me go he called me into his office and told me, "I shall report this matter to the authorities. If your mother can't control your waywardness, it's high time the police were keeping an eye on you."

It was a lucky thing that I suggested the sandwiches to Mother. If I'd come home ten minutes late after she'd told me to hurry, she'd have made me tell her the reason for it, and even though I hadn't really done anything bad, I didn't want her to know I'd had any trouble at school. As it was, it worked out all right. Philip was waiting for me at the corner of Spring and Washington Streets, with his sled, Mother's note, and the bag of sandwiches. By one of us riding and eating while the other ran and pulled the sled, we made up the lost time in going the mile to Medford Square. Of course Philip wanted to know why I was so late, but I just told him that some boy messed things up when we were forming our lines to march out of school. There wasn't any sense in telling him that I was the one.

When we went into the lumberyard office a woman who was writing in some books came over to the counter and asked us what we wanted. Instead of giving her Mother's note, I said, "I want to see your boss. Last week he sent us down some bad lumber and charged us number-one price for it, and now we want . . ."

Before I could tell her we wanted some straight pine boards without any knots in them a big, gray-haired man came out of the little office and said roughly, "What's this you're talking about?"

"Last week you sent us some number nine, ten and eleven lumber, and charged us number-one price for it," I told him.

"Who told you that?" he demanded.

"My Uncle Levi, and he knows," I told him. "Every piece of it was brittle hard pine or hemlock, and it was so crooked that Uncle Levi said it was a wonder your man could get it through a doorway."

"Is that so?" the man said, but his voice wasn't rough when he said it. "Where was it sent to?"

"To Mrs. Moody's, at 46 Spring Street," I said.

"That the old Perkins house?" he asked.

"I suppose so," I told him. "Mr. Perkins is our landlord."

"Well, now," he said, "I recall the order, but I didn't see the stuff that went out on it, or the billing. Miss Northrup, let me see the billing on that Moody order, will you?"

When the woman brought him a copy of the bill that came with our lumber, Mother's first note was pinned to it. After he'd looked at both of them he said, "The order don't specify grade; just calls for three two-by-fours and a dozen one-by-twelves, but the price on the bill is for number one all right. You wait a minute till I find out about it."

He went out to the yard and was gone five or six minutes. When he came back he said, "Sorry, son. They sent number two on that order, and with all the bad weather we've had this winter it might not have been too straight. We'll pick it up and send you some number-one stuff."

"It's too late for that," I told him. "It's already made into a table and a frame for shelves, but we need ten more ten-foot, one-by-twelve, number-one clear white pine boards, and Uncle Frank said . . ."

"Well, now, that's getting right down to specifications," he said. "Did you have all your uncles in on the kill?"

"No, sir," I told him, "only Uncle Levi and Uncle Frank, but . . ."

While I was telling him he began writing figures down on the bill, and he didn't let me finish. "Let's see," he said, sort of to himself, "a hundred foot of clear . . ." Then he looked across the counter at me and asked, "If I called it a dollar fifty for the one-by-twelves could we come out friends?"

"Yes, sir," I told him, "good friends."

He put his big hand across the counter, shook hands with me, and said, "I see you got a sled with you; think you boys can haul the stuff, or want me to send a team down with it?"

"We can haul it all right," I told him, "but we'll have to hurry or we'll be late for school."

Usually my only worry about being late for school was what Mother might say, but that noon I didn't want to risk any more trouble with Mr. Jackman, so we ran as much of the way home as we could. Even with the boards on it, the sled pulled easy where the sidewalks had good hard snow on them, but some people had shoveled their walks too close, and getting the sled across those places was like trying to pull a cow out of a bog.

I slid into my seat at school just as the late bell rang, and I was real careful about marking time when we lined up to go out at half-past three. Mr. Jackman didn't even scowl at me, and I thought he might have forgotten about reporting me to the authorities, but he hadn't. Cop Watson was waiting in the store when I came in for work, and the first thing he said to me was, "What's this report I'm after gettin' about you molestin' the girls at school?"

"I didn't molest any girls," I told him. "I was just marking time when we were waiting to march out, and I happened to lift my knee too high, and it bumped Marion Newell. I guess I was a little closer to her than I thought, and she's sort of fat, and . . ."

Mr. Haushalter slapped both hands down on his thighs and hooted, but Cop Watson looked at him hard, and said, "Molestin' females is no laughing matter at all, at all, Gus, and it's no interference I'll be havin'. Now go on, lad. What was you sayin'?"

"Well," I said, "I guess it kind of scared Marion and she squealed, and . . ."

"Ah, then," he said, "so she tattled on you, did she?"

"No, sir," I told him, "she didn't tattle. In the first place I don't think she would have, and in the second place she didn't need to. Mr. Jackman was right beside her and couldn't help hearing her."

Cop Watson nodded his head and said, "So. So. Then she didn't squeal at all, at all; she hollered."

"Well, it was more of a squeal than a holler," I told him, "but anyway, Mr. Jackman shook the daylights out of me and told me he'd expel me if I ever did it again, and that he was going to report it to the authorities."

"Then he's a man of his word," Cop Watson told me. "The call come into the station house at twelve-naught-seven. Your name's wrote down on the book again, and I've orders to be keepin' a close eye on you. How's Marion feeling about the whole goin's-on?"

"All right, I guess," I told him. "On the way home from school this afternoon she and the other girls were laughing about the way she squealed."

"Then I'm thinkin' there's no call to set up the gallows yet awhile," Cop Watson told me, "but mind your step, lad. Since you poked that principal in the nose, intentional or not, it's no love he has for you, and it goes hard with a lad when he gets his name wrote down three times or more in the bad-boy book. Yours is down twice a'ready. And once it's wrote down, guilty or not, there's no livin' way to get it unwrote."

That night Mother let Philip stay up until ten o'clock to

help me with the new shelves, and I was surprised at what a good carpenter he turned out to be. Of course, our job was an easy one, as compared to the one Uncle Levi and Uncle Frank did on Sunday. The new boards were soft and straight, and the edges were milled so smooth and true that they fitted together without any planing. All we had to do was to lay the boards out on the floor in pairs, mark them by the pattern, saw the ends straight, notch out squares to fit around the uprights, and nail them into place. While I chiseled out the notches, Philip sawed the ends square; for some reason a saw would follow a mark better for him than it would for me. Then we nailed them in place with finish nails that Uncle Levi had left for us, set the nail heads deep, and filled the little holes in with putty. It was just ten o'clock when we finished the job, and Mother said it looked as well as if Uncle Levi had done it himself.

Grace and Mother didn't start their washing until Tuesday morning, and they didn't have to rush with it the way they did the week before. Mrs. Humphrey sent a big basketful, with a note telling Mother to charge her double the regular laundry price for sheets and pillowcases and towels, but Mrs. Sterling sent only stiff bosomed shirts, cuffs, collars and fancy women's clothes.

That Tuesday when I came home for lunch Mother was worried about Mrs. Sterling's bundle being so small, and about the way we were using up our ton of coal. "Good heavens," she said, "that ton of coal is disappearing like dew before the sun! Nearly a quarter of it is gone since Friday, and it cost six dollars. We'll have to keep the fire spanking right along to dry these clothes in the cellar, and it will take just as much coal for this small batch of Mrs. Sterling's as it would for a big batch. My, I shall be thankful when the weather moderates enough that we can dry clothes in the back yard! I wonder, Gracie, if it was wise for me to have written those notes saying that we couldn't afford to do flat work at laundry prices. There'd be an extra dollar in Mrs. Sterling's work, even at laundry prices, if she'd sent all her flat pieces. That would just about pay for the coal we'll burn today and tomorrow."

"I wouldn't worry about it," Gracie told her, "and I wouldn't take any flat work at laundry prices if I were you. If we got ourselves loaded up with that kind of stuff we wouldn't have room or time to handle the fancy work that we hope to get, and we might get the name of doing any old kind of washing."

"I know, Gracie, I know," Mother told her, "but about all we have right now is hope that we'll get more fancy work, and that furnace is eating coal like a steam engine. Maybe if we . . ."

Grace had been biting her teeth hard together, and she sort of exploded when Mother got that far. "But we're not going to!" she said. "With Mrs. Humphrey paying us double for flat work, we'll come out as well this week as we did last, and how can we charge Mrs. Humphrey double and other people only single? And besides, this cold weather isn't going to last forever. Before long we're bound to get a thaw, and until that time comes we can run the furnace only on the days we're drying clothes; the rest of the time the kitchen stove will give us all the heat we really need—if we go to bed early enough."

If I'd talked that way to Mother she'd have sent me right up to my room, but all she said to Grace was, "I suppose you're right, dear, but I hate to think of our living cooped up in a kitchen when we have such a lovely house to enjoy. And, of course, spring will come sooner or later."

18

Daredevil Grace

I T MUST have been the mention of spring that made Mother remember the rubbish we'd carried out of the house and dumped in the back yard. She looked over at me and said, "Son, before this snow melts off and the lawn under it is ruined, we must get rid of all the rubbish we've piled up in our back yard. Do you have any idea as to how we could dispose of it?"

"Sure, I do," I told her. "There's a great big clay pit beyond the field of bushes across the street. It's about a mile deep, and everybody dumps their rubbish into it. I've taken half a dozen loads over there from the store. They don't dig clay out of this pit any more, but from one down near the marshes. This one has a lake in the bottom, and the boys go skating over there when there's no snow on the ice."

"Oh, if it's that deep it must be dangerous," Mother said quickly. "I'd thought Philip might haul some of our rubbish away on his sled, but I couldn't let him go near a place like that."

"I'd be real careful," Philip hurried to tell her, "and I wouldn't have to go right up to the edge. I could dump it farther back, and then push it over the edge with our coal shovel."

"He wouldn't even have to do that," I told her. "It's only in the

170

places where the sides go straight down that it's dangerous. Everybody dumps on the side where they used to take out the clay, and on that side the bank's no steeper than an ordinary roof. If he should fall over the edge he couldn't go five feet before a pile of rubbish would catch him."

"Mmmmm, hmmmm," Mother said. "Maybe I'll let you take him over there and show him where it is tomorrow noon, but don't either of you go near the dangerous side under any circumstances. Now hurry right along with your lunch; Gracie and I must get back to our washing."

I hurried right home from school Wednesday noon, and Philip and I took the first load over to the clay pit. The bushes, as high as a man's head, had kept the snow from drifting in the big field across the street from our house, so we didn't have much trouble in pulling the sled, but when we got to the pit it seemed a shame to dump rubbish into it.

I'd told Mother that the pit was a mile deep, but, of course, that was only talking. The lake was only about two hundred feet below the level of the brush field, and the top rim was almost perfectly round, an eighth of a mile from edge to edge. Most of the way around, the banks dropped almost straight down, but on the south side there was a steep causeway that reached out into the lake a hundred feet or more. Its top cut back through the upper edge of the pit between high clay walls. Al Richardson had told me there used to be a track on the causeway, and that the clay was pulled up to the brick sheds on little cable cars. The blizzard that we'd had must have dumped thousands of tons of snow into the pit, and whirled it around and round the high banks, like egg whites being whipped in a bowl.

Philip and I were the first ones to go there after the storm. There wasn't a footprint anywhere. As we pulled the sled up to the edge I couldn't help catching my breath. It seemed as if we were the tiniest of pygmies, standing on the brim of a great, pure white cup that had been pushed down into the earth. Or maybe it was more like a white cream pitcher, with the causeway making the lip of the spout. The wind had whirled the snow around in such a way that the high, circular walls were completely covered, and the bank of snow at their base curved out to meet the flat field of white that covered the lake. "Let's not dump this stuff over the edge and spoil it," I told Philip. "Let's dump it back here in the bushes, and after the snow is gone we'll come and shovel it over the edge."

Thursday evening was sharp and clear, the snow squeaked under my rubbers as I walked home from work, and the full moon was so bright that, as I went from street light to street light, my shadow walked beside me. Except at the corners where the lights were bright, the shadows of the houses lay black on the white snow, and the bare limbs of the trees seemed to me like arms reaching up toward Heaven in prayer. As soon as I got home I asked Mother to put on her coat and come out to the yard with me, so she could see it.

I think the moonlight must have done about the same thing to Mother that it did to me. When we were finishing supper she said, "Wouldn't this be a glorious evening to go sleigh riding? When Father and I were courting, he used to take me riding whenever we had an evening like this; over the hills, and through the pine woods and birches. I can still hear the singing of the sleigh runners, and the jingling of the bells, and your father's voice as it used to be when we were young."

For a minute or two Mother sat, sort of half-smiling and looking at the picture behind Hal's chair as if she'd forgotten where she was. Then she said quickly, "Why don't you children go sliding tonight, on Philip's new sled? It would be a lovely evening for it."

"There are no hills around here," Grace told her. "The nearest ones are the Fells, but the only place to slide there would be in the streets coming down the hillside, and that's too dangerous. All those streets run into Fellsway Boulevard at the bottom, and automobiles go whizzing along at thirty miles an hour."

"I know a place," I told her. "We could slide over at the clay pit; down the causeway where they used to pull clay up."

"Oh, that would be entirely too dangerous!" Mother said. "I couldn't possibly let you do anything like that."

"Who'd want to slide in a clay pit anyway?" Grace asked. "I certainly wouldn't . . . not even if I was still young enough to go sliding."

"If I were," Mother said, "not, if I was."

"Oh, don't try to be so grown-up," I said to Grace. "You won't be fifteen till next month! And besides, the clay pit would be a good place to slide, and it wouldn't be too dangerous, either. That causeway is as wide as an ordinary wagon road, and it isn't much steeper than some of those streets up at the Fells. If you don't want to go, I'll take Philip and Muriel."

For some reason, Mother didn't say, "No bickering!" when I snapped at Grace, so she yammered right back at me, "Well, go ahead and take them if you want to, but I'm not going to make a spectacle of myself by sliding down into an old clay pit!"

"Oh, no," Mother said, "I can't let Ralph take the children alone. He's entirely too impetuous, and takes too many daring risks. It's a wonder he didn't kill himself in Colorado with some of his trick-riding stunts. No. No. I can't let him take the children alone, but if you were to go along, Gracie, I'd feel perfectly safe about them."

"Well, I'll go if you want me to," Grace told her, "but just to keep an eye on them; I'm not going to do any sliding. And before we start I wish you'd tell Ralph he has to mind me; he gets crazier than a chicken hawk when he's out playing."

"You will do as Gracie tells you, won't you, Ralph?" Mother asked me.

"I will if she doesn't try to get too bossy," I told her, "and if she does, I'll just come home."

"That's all right," Mother said. "Now run along and get your warm clothes on, all of you."

Hal was the first one to say, "Please excuse me," and slide down off his chair, but Mother called him over to her and told him, "We'll have a nice evening of reading, and tomorrow Philip

will take you for a ride on his sled, but you're a little young yet
to go sliding."

Hal pulled himself up onto his tiptoes, so that his chin was
as high as the table, and told her, "I'm big enough now, Mother,
and I've got a warm cap with ear-lappers, and I'll mind everything Grace tells me."

"I know," Mother told him, "but it will probably be way past
your bedtime before the others get home. You can go sometime
when it's daylight, but I'll need you here to keep me company
this evening. I must keep one man in the house, you know." I
thought Hal might cry, but he didn't, and he was helping
Mother clear the table when we left the house.

In the moonlight, the pit was even more beautiful than it
had been in daylight. We followed the path Philip had made in
hauling rubbish, and all the way to the pit Grace acted like an
old hen with a flock of chickens. When we reached the top of
the causeway she wouldn't let us slide down until she'd walked
part of the way to be sure we wouldn't run into anything. Then
she made me sit at the front of the sled, with my feet on the
steering bar. Next she put Muriel, with both arms wrapped
around me, and Philip on the back. She wouldn't give us a
push-off until both Philip and Muriel had their feet tucked up,
or until she'd told me a dozen times over to steer in close to the
wall, and not to dare go anywhere near the steep fall-off.

Grace didn't give us a very good push-off, and the causeway
wasn't awfully steep right at the top, but with every foot we
gained speed, and we must have been going a mile a minute
when we reached the bottom. The steering bar sent snow flying
like a blizzard, and we swooped more than halfway across the
lake before we came to a stop. On our way back we walked three-
abreast, and took short steps, to tramp the snow down and make
a good runway. Grace gave us a better push-off on our second
run. With the steering bar I could keep the sled right in the
middle of the runway, and we were really flying when we hit
the snow field at the bottom. We streaked out across the lake
like a hurricane, hit the end of our first tracks in an explosion of

flying snow, and didn't stop until we'd run part way up the hard-packed drift at the foot of the far wall.

It couldn't have been more than half a minute from the time Grace gave us our push-off until we'd reached the far wall, but it took us at least ten minutes to walk back across the lake and climb the causeway. When we reached the top Grace was flailing her arms around her chest and looked to be about half frozen. "Let me have that thing a minute," she said when I pulled the sled up beside her. "You're wasting most of your time walking back."

Grace stood the sled up in front of her, looped the tow rope back loosely around the center boards, tied it, and stood holding the side bars just above the center. Before I had any idea what she was going to do she ran toward the top of the causeway, dived off over the edge, and landed belly-bump on the sled as it hit the snow. "Look out!" I yelled after her. "You've got to hold onto the cross bar to steer it!"

Bright as the moonlight was, Grace was going so fast that I couldn't see what she was doing with her hands. I could only see that the sled was leaving the runway before it was halfway down the narrow causeway, and that it was veering away from the wall and toward the drop-off. I tried to yell to her to get her hands up on the cross bar to steer it straight, but I was so scared I couldn't make a sound. I could only stand there holding my breath as the sled skimmed along the very edge of the drop-off. Then it veered the other way, right toward the wall, at the top of the hard-packed drift that curved down to the snow field.

I was so sure Grace would be killed that I shut my eyes for a moment, but when I opened them I could see the dark streak of the sled skimming around the high curved wall like a marble being whirled in a cup. The sled seemed to be lying almost on its side as it flew along, clinging to the line where the big drift began to curve out toward the snow field. Scared as I was, I had sense enough to know that a sled couldn't do a thing like that all by itself. Grace had to have hold of the steering bar, and she had to be doing a whale of a fine job of steering. The sled skimmed along until I could see that it was beginning to slow down. Then Grace turned it in a wide curve, came shooting down the curve of the drift, and heading back toward the foot of the causeway. She came the last hundred yards in the runway we'd packed down on our first two slides, and she'd made a good start back up the causeway before the sled came to a stop.

I was running before Grace turned the sled down from the wall, and I reached her a few seconds after she came to a stop. "What in the world did you do that for?" I shouted at her as she bounced to her feet. "It's a wonder you didn't kill yourself!"

She was laughing like a little kid, and mopping the snow off her face. "Wheee, that was fun!" she squealed. "See, I told you you were wasting time! With a sled like this there's nothing to it. I'll betcha I could steer it through a blackberry patch without getting scratched by a sticker. Come on, let's you and I try it together; then we'll slide the children down the straight runway."

Muriel was so scared she was crying, and Philip was shaking all over when we pulled the sled to the top of the causeway. Grace had to lie to them a little, telling them there wasn't the least bit of danger in the stunt she'd pulled, before they got over being scared. Then we took them for a ride down the straight runway, and pulled them back on the sled before Grace and I tackled the circle tour.

"Half of it's in getting a flying start," Grace told me as we stood at the top of the causeway, "and it has to be done belly-bump, so you'll be lying down and can get a good hard pull on the steering bar. There's only one way I can think of for us to be running fast enough and both go belly-bump together. You stand right behind me, and I'll count. One . . . two . . . three. . . . Go! Then, just one step before I'm going to dive, I'll yell Go! again. If you take off as quick as you hear me, we might come down on the sled together. And if we don't what's the odds? We just pile up in the snow and skid a little ways."

Our take-off worked almost the way Grace had planned it, but not quite. I dived the instant I heard her yell, "Go!" But,

without any sled to carry, I probably dived a little bit harder than she did. For a split second I thought I was going to sail clear over her, then we banged down on the sled together, with my chest hitting her right between the shoulder blades. The air went out of her like a puffball that's been stepped on, and the sled slewed crazily for a few yards. Then Grace got her hands on the steering bar and straightened us out, but we didn't miss the edge of the drop-off by more than six inches. I had to hang on with my teeth and toenails as she made the bumpy turn across the straight runway, and then we were skimming along the wall. The sled was laid way over sideways, but instead of feeling as if I might slip off I was pressed down onto Grace harder than ever. It was probably my added weight that made the sled run faster, and it didn't slow enough that Grace could turn it down the curve until we were way beyond the place where she'd turned the first time. Even at that, we came down the curve so fast that we were clear back to the foot of the causeway before we came to a stop.

"Whewwww," Grace whistled as she climbed up off the sled and rubbed her ribs, "you came down on me like a ton of bricks dropped out of the sky. How much candy have you been eating down at the store? I'll bet you've gained ten pounds in just the few weeks you've been working there."

"I might have gained two, but not ten," I told her. "My pants are getting a little tight, and either my shoes have shrunk or my feet are growing. These new ones Mother bought me when we left Colorado squeeze my toes till they feel as if they're freezing half the time and burning the other half."

"Well, there are scales at the store, aren't there? Why don't you weigh yourself?" Grace asked as we pulled the sled up the causeway. "The next time you're going to dive first, and I'll dive on top of you. Then I can reach over your shoulders and help you with the steering till you've done it a time or two."

Grace and I made four more runs of the circle tour, with only a few bobbles, and straight rides in between for Philip and Muriel. If we hadn't been afraid Mother'd be worried about us,

I think we'd have stayed all night, and Grace had as much fun as the rest of us. She forgot all about acting grown-up, didn't try to boss me at all, and was just as happy as she used to be when we were out riding horses and playing follow-the-leader on the ranch.

Mother had been a little worried about us before we got home, but she got all over it as soon as she saw Grace's face. "Oh, Gracie," she said, "I'm so glad you went, and so glad you had so much fun! Wasn't it just like being a little girl again? My, I'd give a cookie if I could go back—just for an evening—and do it all over again. I can remember it as clearly as if it were yesterday: my brother Ralph and I sliding down the long orchard hill behind the barn in the moonlight. Then running to the house for a cup of steaming hot cambric tea with ginger in it. My! My! I haven't tasted cambric tea with ginger in it for nearly thirty years. How about it? Let's make some right now! There's nothing in the world to top off sledding like hot cambric tea with ginger."

We hadn't mentioned the circle tour, but Mother seemed to know without being told. All the time we were drinking our cambric tea she told about the fun she and Uncle Ralph used to have on the old farm, and before she went up to bed she said, "I want you children to go out every evening while this weather holds and the moon is bright, and if you don't stay too late Hal can go along. It will be so soon that you won't be children any longer, and I want you to have all the joy you can to look back to."

We went sliding at the clay pit both Friday and Saturday nights, but we didn't go alone. I guess I talked too much at school. Friday night Al Richardson and half a dozen boys were over there with their sleds. By Saturday the whole causeway was packed into a hard runway, and half the kids in our end of Medford were at the pit, but only four or five of them had courage enough to try the circle tour. A few tried to do it with ordinary bobsleds, but they couldn't even make the first turn, and most of them tumbled head-over-heels down the drop-off.

Philip let Al Richardson and several of the boys borrow his *Flexible Flyer* for trying the circle tour, but most of them lost their nerve when it came time to turn in against the wall. Al was the only one, beside Grace and me, who could make the whole swing.

On Sunday, of course, we couldn't slide, and by Monday the February thaw had set in.

19

New Customers

GRACE was right in her guess that I was beginning to grow again. I'd weighed seventy-two pounds before Father died, in 1910, and I still weighed seventy-two pounds when I got the job in the D & H Grocery at the beginning of 1912. But by the end of February I was up to eighty pounds, and Mother said she believed I'd grown an inch taller. I don't think it was the candy that did it, because I'd only eaten a piece or two a day —after the first week. But it might have been because Mr. Haushalter brought me a big piece of cheese and a handful of crackers almost every day. Or it might have been that I'd ridden too many rough horses while we lived in Colorado, or that the altitude was too high for my leaky heart. Whatever it was, I must have started growing from the first day I went to work in the store.

But Mother was losing weight a lot faster than I was gaining. Most of it, I think, was more from worry than hard work. Each week she and Grace had Mrs. Humphrey's and Mrs. Sterling's laundry to do, and each week it brought in about eight dollars, but she didn't get any new customers. Then, too, the whole month of March was cold and blustery. We'd have a thaw for a day or two, then it would turn cold again, and we had one real blizzard. Our first ton of coal lasted only until the first of the month, and we'd burned two more before April Fool's Day. On days when there was washing to be dried I had to keep the furnace fire high, but on the other days I kept it banked with cinders, and the house just warm enough at night that the water pipes wouldn't freeze.

Before March was over we were having baked beans four or five times a week, and meat only on Sundays. Grace and I knew that Mother was as near being discouraged as we'd ever seen her, but she would never mention it and, of course, we didn't either. Only those who knew Mother as well as Grace and I did could ever have guessed that things weren't going along fine for us. At church she was even more pleasant than usual, and when Mr. Vander Mark asked her how she was getting on, she said, "Splendidly, Doctor; splendidly! The children have all fitted right into their new schools nicely, and our laundry customers seem well satisfied with our work. As soon as we've picked up one or two more, I shall feel that our little business is well established."

Mrs. Humphrey and Mrs. Sterling were at church every Sunday, and each time they visited with Mother a few minutes after the service. Two or three times I heard one or the other of them tell her they had recommended her work to some of their friends, but that was as much as we had ever heard about any new customers.

The first Sunday in April Grace asked me to go for a walk with her as soon as dinner was over. We were barely out of sight from the house when she told me, "I'm going to find myself a job. Tomorrow I want you to find me some excuse for being away from home for a few hours; somebody's baby to tend, or something like that. And then I want you to tell it to me at the table when you come home for lunch. That way it won't be a lie, because I'll already know it isn't so, and you won't be lying to Mother because you'll be talking to me, and she'll just be overhearing it."

"That wouldn't work," I told her. "Where would you find a job in a few hours that would pay as much as you make by helping with the business we already have? You remember how hard and how long Mother hunted for work before she found any, don't you?"

"Sure I do, and I remember where she found it, too. I can now iron stiff-bosomed shirts and collars and cuffs, and other fancy things as well as anybody else. And if Mother could get a laundry job without experience, I'll bet I can get one with."

"You're not going to do anything of the kind!" I told her. "About all you'd have to do would be to walk through Edgeworth a couple of times, alone and after dark, and you'd be a gone goose. I'm going to quit school and go to work full-time. Even if they don't need me full-time at the store, the man in the lumberyard is my friend. We shook hands and said so, and I'll bet he'd give me a job anytime—and maybe for as much as four dollars a week. That's pretty near as much as you'd make in the laundry if you had to pay carfare both ways."

"Don't be silly!" Grace told me. "You're a boy, and boys have to get an education if they're going to amount to anything. You could do Mother more good by staying in school till you've learned enough to hold down a better job than working in a lumberyard. You still try to spell cat with a K."

When Grace had her head set on something it took more than me to stop her, so I didn't argue any more, but she got stopped anyhow. That Sunday afternoon Mother read to us for a little while, but she couldn't seem to keep her mind on her reading, and she lost her place two or three times. The parlor wasn't really cold, but it was sort of chilly, and once Mother told me to go down and open the furnace drafts a little. But before I got as far as the kitchen she called me back and told me to never mind, that we'd have to make this last ton of coal stretch just as far as it would go. She read another page or two, lost her place again, and then said, "Why don't we all go to church this evening? I don't know what it is, but something keeps telling me that we ought to go. Elizabeth would sleep very nicely in my arms, and if Hal should go to sleep I'm sure no one would mind."

It wasn't too much warmer in the church than it was in our own parlor, but Mr. Vander Mark preached a real good sermon and I was glad we were there. I was even more glad when the sermon was over. As we walked down the aisle I noticed that Mrs. Humphrey was standing by the vestibule door, talking to two ladies I didn't remember having seen at church before. We had nearly reached them when Mrs. Humphrey looked up and said, "Oh, Mrs. Moody, you're just the one I'm looking for! I'd like you to meet some friends of mine."

Grace took Elizabeth out of Mother's arms, and we went on to the vestibule while she stopped to be introduced. Almost everyone had left the church before Mother came out, and she looked ten years younger than she had when she went in. She didn't say a word until we were well away from the church, but Grace poked me with her elbow and nodded. Neither of us was much surprised when Mother said, "My, those were charming ladies! And they're both going to try our work. The taller one was Mrs. Nickerson, the wife of our Superintendent of Schools. Philip, with four baskets to be picked up tomorrow afternoon, you'll have to hurry right straight home from school."

"Now that all the snow is gone, he won't be able to use his sled," I told Mother, "so I guess I'd better ask Al Richardson if we can borrow his cart. He has a good one, almost new, that he uses for his morning paper route, but his evening route is light enough that he doesn't really need a cart for it."

"No!" Mother said. "No, we are not going to be borrowers! If you boys hurry right home from school tomorrow noon you will have plenty of time to pick up Mrs. Humphrey's basket. It won't be so heavy but what you should be able to carry it, and the other three will doubtlessly be light enough that Philip and Muriel can manage with them. If these new customers should prove to be profitable ones, we will have to consider buying a cart of our own. I wonder how much they cost."

"Three ninety-five," I told her. "That's what Al's cost, and it's a good one."

"My!" Mother said. "That's quite a lot of money! But then, we can't run a business without equipment, and we will need a good sturdy cart. Well, that's a bridge we'll have to cross when we come to it. For the present you children will just have to carry the baskets by hand."

"Well," I said, "if I can find a dump where there's an old baby carriage with good wheels, I could get a big box and make . . ."

"No," Mother told me. "No, Son! If we are going to run a first-class business we must have first-class equipment. We'll simply have to wait about a cart until we see how these new customers are going to work out. You know, they might send us only a very few garments at the beginning. Now let's hurry right along. With a big week's work before us, we must all go right to bed and get our rest."

Except for the first week, when we had the big blizzard, Mrs. Humphrey's basket had never seemed to be terribly heavy. And, with the sled to carry it on, the half-mile from her house to ours had never seemed very far. But before Philip and I got her basket home that Monday noon the distance seemed like ten miles, and the basket dragged down on our arms as if it had been filled with rocks. We had to rest at every corner, and it took us so long that I had to run all the way to school to keep from being late.

We couldn't have been the only people in Medford who'd had to spend more money than they'd expected to for coal that winter, or who had been eating baked beans during March. When I went to work that Monday afternoon, there were half a dozen customers in the store, one whole side of the floor was lined up with filled grocery baskets, and Mr. Durant was still putting up orders. I pitched right in to help Mr. Haushalter with the customers, and when we both had to go back to the kerosene barrel at the same time, I asked him, "Where did all the business come from?"

"First of the month," he told me, "and folks has got their pay checks. With April here they ain't savin' out much for coal, and I calc'late they're fed up on beans. Always comes about this way after a hard winter. You hyper along and get them baskets took out for John; I'll take care of the store trade."

I was so busy for the next couple of hours that I didn't have any time to think about home, or about anything else except pumping the old bicycle as fast as I could make it go. I'd delivered an order, way over on the Fellsway, and was hurrying back to the store when I saw Philip and Muriel about a block ahead of me. They were trying to carry a basket that was bigger than both of them put together, and were having to set it down every five or six steps. I couldn't stop to help Philip home with the basket, but I took nearly half of the laundry ahead on the bike.

I was a little late in getting home from work that night because of all the grocery baskets I had to deliver, and when I came in supper was on the table. Mother didn't say a word about business until I'd asked the blessing and served the plates. Then she looked up at me and asked, "Ralph, do you know where Al Richardson bought his cart?"

"Yes, ma'am," I told her, "at the hardware store at Medford Square. They have nearly a dozen of them, all lined up by the wall; some blue and some red and some brown."

"Mmmm, hmmm," Mother hummed. "If I were to have sandwiches ready when you come home from school tomorrow noon, do you think you boys would have time to run up there and buy us one? That is, if they're good and sturdy. Philip will need a good sturdy cart if we're to continue getting these heavy baskets."

20

Never Pick on an Alderman's Son

THE cart Philip and I picked out was a good one—red—and it really didn't cost us anything. Tuesday was a bright, warm day, and when we came home with the cart Mother was hanging out clothes in the back yard. After we'd talked about the cart for a minute or two, she said, "My, isn't this a lovely day! Spring is really in the air, and it always makes my fingers itch to get into the soil. We must get our garden started right away. If we could manage to raise ourselves a good crop of vegetables this summer we'd save many a dollar on our grocery bill."

The yard behind our house was a big one, and the lawn went only halfway to the back fence. Anyone who had ever been a farmer could see that the space beyond the lawn had once been a garden, but that it hadn't been planted for several years, and that the soil wasn't very fertile. The dried weed stalks from the year before were spindly, and even the witch grass was thin and wirelike. "I'm afraid we wouldn't get very much of a crop without at least two loads of good barnyard dressing," I told Mother. "Don't you notice how spindly the old weeds are? With as much rain as they have here those stalks ought to be as big around as your thumb, so the land must be pretty well worn out."

Mother looked at the dried weeds for a minute and said, "I'm afraid you're right, Son, but a good garden will be well worth a little expense. Doesn't Mr. Young, the man who delivered our furniture for us, keep cows and sell dressing?"

"Yes, ma'am," I told her, "but it costs a lot of money. Al's father got a load for their roses, and it cost two dollars and a quarter."

"Oh, my!" Mother said. "Two dollars and a quarter! Why, when I was a child . . ." She seemed to have forgotten what she was going to say, and just stood looking at the big oblong of brown, sandy loam. "Hmmmm, that would be four dollars and a half for two loads," she said at last, "and the seed would doubtlessly cost another dollar, but a good garden would be worth much more than five fifty to us. Though I hate to spend the money right now, a garden is something that can't wait. The peas should already be in the ground, and within a week the soil will be warm enough for string beans and turnips and carrots. Tomorrow noon you might drop by Mr. Young's house, Ralph, and tell him we'd like two loads of dressing as soon as he can deliver it."

"Now that we have a cart I think I know how we can do better than that," I told her. "Lots of people around here keep hens, and they have to keep them in coops all winter, and in the spring the coops have to be cleaned out, and I'll bet almost anybody would give the dressing for getting their hencoop cleaned out!"

"Oh, not with the new cart we're going to use for delivering clean laundry!" Mother said.

"It wouldn't hurt the cart," I told her. "We'd take boxes along, lined with newspaper, and I'll bet we wouldn't spill a crumb in the cart."

"We'll talk about it more tonight," Mother said, "but you boys had better run right along to school so you won't be late."

Philip and I walked as far as the James School together, and he thought my idea about hencoops was a good one, but he was

sure Mother wouldn't let us do it. "Well, she didn't say positively no," I told him, "and if we should try it and it should happen to work out all right, she might never say it at all. Why
don't you go over and ask Mrs. Hutchinson about her hencoop
right after school? They have quite a few hens and no garden.
If she says all right, you could tell her that we'll clean it right
after supper. I don't think Mother would talk about dressing at
the table, so we might get the job all done before she knows
anything about it."

Philip was so anxious to use his new cart that he didn't wait
for me to help him. The minute school was out he went over to
see Mrs. Hutchinson, and when she told him it would be all
right he started to work on her hencoop. By the time I came
home from work he had the job all finished, and about four
bushels of good dressing piled up in our garden. All Mother
said about it was, "My, that ought to make us a nice fertile
garden!"

By the end of the week Philip had cleaned four more hencoops, all by himself. Our garden had all the dressing it needed,
and we had more than half of it planted.

With one exception, April was about the luckiest month we
ever had. Mother got two more customers, our garden grew to
beat the band, and Grace's cake won first prize at the Sunday
School picnic on Lexington Day. The exception was my getting
my name down on the bad-boy book again, and it wasn't really
my fault. After we got our cart Philip and Muriel picked up all
the baskets of laundry and made the deliveries. He always
pulled the cart and she walked beside it, to steady the basket
and the boxes of fancy things when they had to go up and down
over curbs. They'd never had any trouble, but when I knew
they had a big load, I tried to keep an eye on them a bit. Of
course, I couldn't do it all the time, but if I was out delivering
an order I'd ride the bike a little out of my way to use streets I
knew they'd be following.

The week before the Sunday School picnic Mrs. Humphrey
sent a big basketful, with lots of fancy things in it, so when it

was finished Grace had to pack it in six or seven suit boxes. We had several customers in the store when Philip and Muriel went past with the delivery, but I noticed that they were having some trouble with slipping boxes when they crossed Spring and started up Washington Street. Between customers I kept an eye on them as they went up Washington, and when they turned out of sight down Otis Street I began to worry about them. As soon as we'd taken care of all the customers I asked Mr. Haushalter if I could take the bicycle and ride up to see how Philip and Muriel were getting along.

Except for getting my name down on the book again, it was lucky that I went. When I turned the corner at Otis, Philip and Muriel were only halfway down the block, and they were having plenty of trouble. Three boys were laughing and shouting as they knocked boxes off the cart, Philip and Muriel were both trying to push them away, but with three against two they weren't doing any good. Just as I got there one of the boys grabbed the side of the cart and tipped it over, spilling the whole basketful of clean laundry out into the street.

I was so mad I was seeing red, and the boys were so busy they didn't see me coming. Maybe that's how I managed to get in as many good licks as I did, right at the start. The boys were all bigger than we were, and in a fair fight they could have licked us easy enough, but that wasn't a fair fight: I didn't tell them, "Put your fists up!" before I swung, Philip kicked one of them in the shins, and Muriel used a stick. Of course, a girl couldn't have been expected to fight with her fists, and the stick Muriel picked up wasn't much bigger than a ruler, but she waded into those boys as if she were swinging a sword. And Philip couldn't be blamed very much for kicking. He'd never been in a real fight before, there were two boys punching at him, and he was just fighting back with everything he had.

I don't think the whole fight lasted more than two minutes, but it was plenty hot while it did last. And it was the bicycle that really stopped it. I didn't have time to stand it up against a tree when I got there, but just jumped off and let it fall in the street. Then I went mainly after the boy who had tipped the cart over. He was a little bigger than the other two, and as I fought with him he tried to angle around so he could tramp on the spilled clothes. But Muriel beat him away with her stick, and I kept punching at his face and stomach until I had him going backwards.

If you can keep the one you're fighting going backwards he can't get set to punch very hard, and you can get in some real good licks. I did, and with every one he kept going faster until his feet got tangled up in the front wheel of the bicycle. When he started to fall he twisted around to save himself, but he didn't get his hands up quick enough, and landed face-down on the brick paving. I'd bloodied his nose and got a good sock into one eye before he fell, but whatever I hadn't done to his face, the bricks did. And they took all the fight out of him. Before I could get around the bike he scrambled to his feet, bawling, and ran toward Central Avenue. And the other boys ran after him.

Until the fight was over neither Philip nor I knew that we'd been hit, or that ladies on both sides of the street were standing on their front piazzas, shouting for us to stop. As soon as the boys had gone the ladies came running to help us pick up the clothes, and to see how much we had been hurt. One of them told me if I'd pinch my nose tight for a minute it would stop bleeding, and another wiggled Philip's front teeth to see if they were loosened enough that he ought to go to a dentist. There's one thing I'll have to say for those boys: they didn't hit Muriel, but they couldn't have missed Philip's face or mine with many punches. We were both a little messed up, and three spokes were broken out of the front wheel of the D & H bicycle.

Of course, there was nothing we could do but take the mussed and dirty laundry home. I didn't stop at the store, because I didn't want to tell Mr. Haushalter about the bicycle right then, or to have him see me looking the way I did. Mother didn't scold me at all for getting into the fight, and Grace said for us not to feel bad about their having to do most of the laundry over again. She held a cold, wet cloth against my eye, so it wouldn't turn too black, and she was real careful not to hurt my nose when she washed the blood off it.

It was nearly an hour before I'd taken a bath, changed my clothes and got back to the store. I hadn't finished telling Mr. Haushalter that I was sorry about the bicycle, and that I'd pay for getting it fixed, when Cop Watson came in. "So it's another fight you've been in," he said to me, and he said it as if he had come to arrest me.

"Yes, sir," I told him, "but it wasn't my fault."

"Divil a bit, it wasn't!" he said. "It was you what flung the first punch, wasn't it?"

"Yes, sir," I said, "but I had to. There were three boys knocking boxes off our laundry cart, and one of them tipped it over."

"Ah, go on with you! Don't be givin' me none o' your fairy tales!" he said roughly. "They was walkin' down the street and your brother and sister was takin' up the whole sidewalk with their wagon, and when the boys tried to squeeze past a box tumbled off, so you come up from behind and go to slingin' fists and beatin' 'em with a club."

"I didn't either!" I told him. "I didn't have a thing in my hands, and I wouldn't have hit them if they hadn't knocked the boxes off the cart and tipped it over on purpose."

I was standing behind the counter with Mr. Haushalter, and Cop Watson came over and leaned on it. He bent over and looked right into my good eye for a minute, not hard, but just steady. Then he said, "Lad, you're in trouble up to your neck, and 'twill only go harder with you if you lie about it. One o' the boys has a'ready been up to the station house with his old man, and the chief's after tellin' me the poor lad's face is beat to a pudd'n'. And that's not all, at all. There's a lump the size of a baseball on the top of his noggin, and a welt acrost the side of his jaw where he was beat with a club."

"Then he's the one that tipped the wagon over," I told Cop Watson, "and he's the one I saw knock the first box off the cart. But I didn't hit him with a club, and if his face is all beat to a pudding it's because he landed on it when he fell over the bicycle. He was the one that started the trouble, not me! And if you don't believe me you ask any of those ladies up on Otis Street. There were three or four of them standing on their front piazzas and shouting for us to stop fighting."

I don't think Cop Watson believed me even then, but Mr. Haushalter helped me out by telling him he'd never caught me lying, and that I'd never acted quarrelsome.

"Well, I'll mosey up the line and have a word with the ladies," Cop Watson told him, "but mind you, Gus, this is no small offense at all, at all, and I can't be brushin' it over easy. The chief's het up like a teakettle. And don't be forgettin': the lad's name has been wrote down in the book twice before this time. You keep him here in the store till I get back; I might be havin' to take him up to the station house."

Just as Cop Watson was going out the doorway, Mr. Haushalter called to him and asked, "Who were they, kids from around the neighborhood?"

Cop Watson turned and told him, "No. From Edgeworth, bad cess to 'em. And, worst of all, it had to be an alderman's son what got the tar pasted out of him."

He started to go on out, then turned back again and told me, "If ever you hit a kid again, for glory's sake pick on a President's son; an alderman can make it forty times as rough on you."

I watched Cop Watson all the way up Washington Street, until he turned the corner at Otis. And I was still watching an hour later when he turned the corner to come back. He wasn't hurrying, but walking with his head down, and his flat feet made him roll a bit from side to side as he came. I didn't want to have him take me up to the station house, and with every slow step he took my heart seemed to beat faster.

"Well, lad," he told me when he came into the store, "you've got them ladies' sympathy all right, all right, but that's all you've got; and sympathy'll never, never in the world rub your name off of that book. There wasn't a livin' one o' them seen the start of it. When they heard the hollerin' and run out the fight was on, but they've cleared you of wieldin' the club. That little sister of yours must be a Tartar when her dander's up. I'll not be takin' you up to the station house when I go in to report, but stay to home this evenin'; I'll maybe drop by for a word with your mother."

As Cop Watson talked to me he took out his jackknife, opened it, and whittled a chew off his plug of B-L. After he'd tucked it away in his cheek, he looked at some notes he had in his helmet, brushed his big white mustache back with a hand, and started out. With one foot on the doorstep, he turned back to me and said gently, "For glory's sake, lad, watch your step." Then he went out, and I had to swallow hard, because my throat hurt.

I told Mother all about Cop Watson when I went home from work, and that he'd probably come to our house to talk to her about me, but I didn't tell her that my name had already been down on the bad-boy book twice before. I didn't want to worry her, and I was sure I could keep it from ever being written down again.

That evening Mother read to Grace and me till after ten o'clock while we were waiting for Cop Watson, but he didn't come, and she kissed me when I went upstairs to bed.

21

Fire!

SOMETIMES when I thought I'd had the worst luck of anybody in the whole world there would be some good come of
it. That's the way it turned out about our having the fight with
the boys from Edgeworth. I found that I had a lot more friends
at school than I'd known about. From that time on they kept
an eye on Philip and Muriel when they were delivering laundry, and no kids from Edgeworth or anywhere else ever dared
to tip over our cart again.

It was only a couple of weeks after the fight that Medford
had one of its biggest fires, and that was when it really helped
me to have so many new friends. Our house was right next to
the Glenwood Fire Station, and we were eating supper when
we heard the horses clattering out of their stalls to take their
places in front of the engine. Before the alarm sounded they
were racing down Spring Street toward Riverside Avenue.

That evening the bell kept tolling and tolling, but it was no
combination for a district in our end of town, and I couldn't
understand why our engine had gone out. At last I asked Mother
if I might be excused, and went out on the front piazza to look
around. The sky to the southeast was so red that the full moon

looked to be floating in a sea of blood above the marshes, halfway between Wellington and Somerville.

At first I was sure I must be wrong about the location, because there were no houses within half a mile of the Mystic River, and the marsh grass was too green to burn. While I was standing there trying to figure it out I heard the clanging of two more fire engines, and the pounding of horses' hoofs as they galloped eastward along Riverside Avenue, going from Medford Square toward the Fellsway. No matter what it was, I knew it had to be an awfully big fire to call out every engine in town, so I ran back into the house and asked Mother if I could go.

"Oh, no, Son!" she told me. "You're entirely too impetuous to be running off to a big fire after dark."

"I'd be real careful," I told her, "and I wouldn't go too close."

"No," Mother said. "With your name on the police book, deservedly or not, I can't let you run off alone to a fire."

"Well," Grace told her, "I'd go with him if you want me to, just to see that he doesn't get into any trouble, but it can't amount to much if it's out in the middle of the marshes."

"Run along then," Mother told her, "but don't be gone more than an hour."

Until we were away from the house Grace didn't hurry, but just as soon as we were out of sight she ran so fast it kept me winded to stay abreast of her. When we'd passed the brickyards on Riverside Avenue, we could see yellow flames leaping high into the red glow above them, and they were coming from the Wellington Bridge, where Fellsway Boulevard crossed the Mystic River. It was a wooden bridge, about a quarter of a mile long, with a pair of streetcar tracks in the middle and a wide roadway on both sides.

There seemed to be a hundred policemen holding the crowd back from our end of the bridge, and keeping the Fellsway open so fire engines from Malden and Everett and Reading and Winchester could get through. Grace and I got closer to the fire than most people because we picked our way out through the marshes to a dry hummock right at the edge of the mud flats. From there we could see the whole length of the bridge, clear over to the south end where the Charlestown and Somerville firemen were swarming onto the bridge like ants.

The fire must have started in the engine room, right in the middle of the bridge, where they lifted the big spans to let boats go through. And it was so hot the firemen couldn't get close to it. To keep the whole bridge from burning down, they were tearing out a section on both sides, back a hundred feet or so from the flames, and letting the planks and timbers fall into the river.

At the time Grace and I reached the hummock the incoming tide was running strong, and the river was spread out nearly to the top of the mud flats. That didn't worry us, because the top of our hummock was hard, dry clay, so we knew that the tide never came in high enough to cover it.

Of course we knew what a terrible thing a fire was, and what a terrible waste of money, but just the same it was fun to sit there on our hummock watching the crackling, roaring flames, and seeing the geysers of water squirting up from the Boston fire boats, and from half a dozen fire engines at either end of the bridge. The engines from every town on our side of Boston were there, lined up on the bridge where they could pump water out of the river and onto the flames. Under the arch of the feathery streams, between the engines and the fire, a hundred or more firemen were running back and forth on rows of great timbers; prying them loose from the piling and letting them fall into the river.

The bridge had been built with heavy planking across the big timbers, and the roadways paved with wooden blocks that had been soaked in creosote. By the time Grace and I reached our hummock most of the planks and paving blocks had been ripped off, and the tide was floating them up the river past us. Half a dozen firemen would run out onto a girder that was twenty-five or thirty feet long, balance themselves as they reached under to pry it loose from the piling, then race back before it toppled into the river with a splash.

Some of the timbers were caught for a few minutes between the long rows of pilings, but the rising tide always turned them, and the wind drifted them toward our side of the river as they floated upstream through the red glare on the water. I told Grace they looked like an armada of enemy submarines sneaking up the Mystic River to attack Medford.

"Well, I wish some of them would sneak into our cellar," she told me. "If we had half a dozen of those big timbers they'd make us firewood enough to last all next winter, and if we could burn chunks off them in the furnace it would save us two or three tons of coal."

"Maybe I can get some," I said. "They're just throwing them away, so they don't belong to anybody."

"Hmmmfff!" Grace sniffed. "Don't be so silly! Can't you see how high the water splashes when they fall? They must weigh a couple of tons apiece. How do you think a little boy like you

would ever get one of them out of the river, let alone lugging it clear up to our house?"

"Well, I'll betcha I'd find some way to do it," I told her. "I could tie one to stakes on the bank, and saw it into pieces, and haul the pieces home on Philip's cart."

"You'd better forget about the whole business," Grace told me, "and we'd better get home before Mother worries herself to death about us. We've already been here more than an hour."

It wasn't until Grace said we'd better go home that we noticed our hummock had become an island. The water had risen all around it, and stretched for more than a hundred feet back through the eel grass. We had to take off our shoes and stockings to wade back to the Fellsway, and we had to go real slowly, feeling for each step before we took it. Under the water there were deep pot holes of soupy mud, where we could have drowned in a minute if we made a misstep.

Mother didn't scold us for getting home late, because Grace explained about the trouble we'd had getting off the hummock, but she did tell us to go straight to bed. It couldn't have been much later than nine o'clock when I went up to bed, but I couldn't go to sleep for thinking about all that good firewood drifting up the river. I must have stayed awake till way after midnight, thinking about it, and before I went to sleep I had an idea.

The next noon when I was coming home from school Cop Watson was standing at the railroad crossing on Spring Street, talking to the gatekeeper. I didn't want to interrupt, so I just stood there for a minute. When he looked around and saw me, he leaned over and said, "Glory be! You ain't been in another fight, have you? That last shiner you got is still green around the edges."

"No, sir," I told him, "and I'm not going to get in any more, but I wanted to ask you a question."

"If it's havin' to do with the law I might be able to tell you," he said, "but if it's about keepin' your name offa that book you'll have to be figurin' it out for yourself; it's beyond me."

"Well, it's about the law," I told him. "I don't want to do anything to get into more trouble, but I'd like to get some of those planks the firemen ripped off Wellington Bridge last night. They let them fall into the river, and we had a flood tide last night, so some of them must be stranded on the marshes. Would it be all right if I took some of them home for firewood?"

"There's nothin' in the law agin it," he told me, "but you'll never, never in the world lay hands on any one of 'em. Every man jack in town that's loose for the day or out of work has been down there luggin' 'em off since the crack o' dawn. There's naught left but the heavy timbers, and there's naught but a derrick barge could salvage 'em. They was drove out o' the channel by the wind, and every livin' one o' them is stranded in the eel grass above the marge o' the mud flats, where a horse would sink down to his belly and a man to his knees. Forty men couldn't budge one of 'em an inch. I was down there this morn, and 'tis a cryin' shame to see all that good firewood goin' to waste, but there's naught can be done about it. 'Twill still be layin' there when you're as old as me, lest its rotted away in the meanwhiles."

I started to go home to lunch, but I'd only gone half a block when I had an idea and went back to talk to Cop Watson again. He watched me coming toward him, but didn't say anything till I was standing right in front of him. Then he leaned over and asked, "And now what kind o' bug have you got up your sleeve?"

"None," I told him, "I just wanted to ask you something about tides. You see, we didn't have an ocean in Colorado, so I don't know much about them."

"Mmmm, I've heard tell they didn't have no ocean out there," he said. "And what would you be wantin' to know about tides?"

"Is there any telling when we'll have another flood one, like the one we had last night?" I asked him.

"Of course there's tellin'," he said. "Didn't they learn you that in school? When the spring and fall moon's at full there's always a flood tide."

"Thank you very much," I told him. "Then we'll get another flood tide when the moon is full this fall?"

"Ah, go 'long with you!" he said. "Don't they learn you kids nothin' in Colorado? Flood tides don't just come out of no place. They keep gettin' higher and higher as the moon waxes towards the full, and lower and lower as it peters off towards the wane."

"Then we'll have another flood tide at about eight o'clock tonight?" I asked him.

He nodded and said, "But not up to the one o' last night; the moon's commencin' to wane."

"And how about the morning tide, when there isn't any moon," I asked him, "will that be a flood too?"

He nodded again, and I started to run for home, but I'd only gone as far as the first corner when he called me back. He leaned down and shook a finger right in front of my nose. "I'm commencin' to get a smell o' that bug you got up your sleeve," he told me, "but if you're smart you'll keep him hid for a bit. If ever word gets out o' what you're thinkin' about, by morn there wouldn't be a livin' one o' them timbers left on the marshes. Every man jack in town would be down there tonight, floatin' 'em adrift and towin' 'em to a beach where he could saw them up."

"But if I got them adrift before they found out about it, and put my name on each one, and tied it to a stake out on the mud flats, could they still take them?" I asked him.

"Law o' salvage! Law o' salvage!" he told me. "What's turned adrift and abandoned belongs to him that salvages it, and the law will protect him on it, but how is the law goin' to protect a man with forty-'leven timbers staked out on a couple o' miles o' mud flats? 'Twould take more officers than Medford's got on the whole livin' force, and you know the chief don't feel too kindly towards a boy what's got his name wrote down on the book three times. But what would you be wantin' with forty-'leven o' them big timbers? Time you got 'em sawed up and fetched home you'd be an old man."

"Well, I wasn't planning to get them all; just some of them," I told him. Then I ran home as fast as I could go, because I knew Mother would have lunch waiting.

It was Friday noon when I talked to Cop Watson about the tides, and on my way back to school I stopped in at the store to ask Mr. Haushalter if he thought it would be all right for Philip to work in my place for a good part of Saturday. I didn't tell him just what I was going to try to do, but I did tell him that I had a very special job to do that might take most of the day, and I thought it was one that would save Mother as much as twelve dollars or more next winter. At first he would only josh with me, telling me that if I had that sort of a job lined up he wished I'd look around and see what I could find for him, because the store business hadn't been very profitable for the past few years. He kept joshing me so long that I had to run all the way to school, but before I left he told me it would be all right for Philip to work in my place.

I'd hoped I'd have time to talk to some of the boys at school that noon, but I didn't. And, of course, I couldn't talk to them at recess, because I didn't have any recesses. But I got sixteen of the biggest ones together just as soon as school let out, and asked how many of them could swim. When they all said they could, I asked how many would be willing to help me make a dollar the next day if I'd help him make that much too. Then I explained that I was really asking each one separately, and that I'd get as much out of the job as all those who helped me put together. Some of the boys said yes right away, but a few wanted to know what the job was before they'd say it. "Well, right now it has to be a secret or none of us would make anything out of it," I told them. "But I can tell you this much: it's a job that Cop Watson says forty men wouldn't be able to do, and I'll bet we're smart enough to do it without any help."

Maybe it was the "smart enough" that made them all say they wanted to do it, but anyway they said it. So I told them all to meet me at our house at seven o'clock Saturday morning, and to bring their swimming trunks and lunches, a piece of stout rope, a bean pole, and a piece of six-inch board.

Six or seven of the boys walked from the schoolhouse to the store with me, sort of hoping I might tell my best friends what the job was going to be, but I only had time to talk to Al Richardson and Allie Dion. Allie was my best friend, next to Al, and his older brother had a wholesale candy business. He had the two finest horses anywhere around our end of town, and a wagon fitted up with shelves inside for the boxes of candy and gum. The wagon was a beauty, but it wasn't all new. Allie had told me that the running gear was new the fall before, but that a body like that never wore out.

I didn't give two whoops about the candy wagon right then, but I did want to know if Allie's brother still had the old running gear. When Allie said it was still standing out behind their barn I told him I'd give him a quarter if I could use it for doing part of the job I had lined up. It didn't take him two seconds to say that for a quarter I could use it as much as I wanted to. But when I mentioned the horses he said there wouldn't be any use in even asking his brother, because he wouldn't let a soul on earth touch those horses except himself. Allie wanted to tell me a lot more about his brother and the horses, but we were getting pretty close to the store, and I wanted to talk to Al alone, so I just said, "So long, Allie. See you at my house in the morning."

I knew I could trust Al with any kind of a secret, so I told him what I was planning to do and how I thought we could do it. Then I asked him where there was the best and shallowest beach along the river.

"There's only one," he told me, "and it isn't very shallow. It's at the end of Foster's Court, just off Riverside Avenue, and at flood tide the water comes almost up to the roadway."

"How deep is the sand?" I asked him.

"That's the trouble with Foster's Beach," he said, "there isn't any sand. It's all hard gravel, and in the spring when your feet are tender. . . ."

"So much the better," I told him, "but I'll be late for work if I don't hurry. Remember to bring a sharp hatchet, and we'll need a couple of pieces of heavy chain, five or six feet long."

I didn't think it would be best to tell Mother all about what I was planning to do, but while we were eating supper I told her about the paving blocks and what good kindling they'd make. Then I told her that if Philip could work in my place I thought I could pick up as many as ten bushels, and that a few other boys were coming by our house in the morning to pick up blocks too.

All she said was, "It would be wonderful to have the kindling, but you'll have to make your deal with Philip." And, of course, that was easy.

22

The Law of Salvage

By FIVE minutes of seven Saturday morning the boys were all gathered out in front of our house. While we were walking down to the marshes I told them how I thought we could get the big timbers that were stranded in the eel grass, that high tide would be at 9:26, and that we'd have to hurry to be ready for it. First we'd hide our clothes in the old abandoned brick shed, far out on the marshes. Then everybody would scatter out through the eel grass along the river, hunting for the timbers. Whenever anybody found one he'd stick up a pole or a board beside it, and hang his shirt or handkerchief on top. Then, when we had them all marked, we'd decide which ones would be easiest to get into the river.

Finding the timbers and marking them was a harder job than I had thought it would be. We had to wade through muck up to our knees, and the sharp eel grass cut our feet and legs like hacksaw blades. But by half-past-eight we had shirts and handkerchiefs hanging from poles and boards for more than half a mile along the river margin. Some of them were no more than a few yards back from the mud flat, but others were as much as eighty or ninety feet.

I could count twenty-six flags when I called the boys together. I told them that the flood tide would last only a half-hour, so we couldn't take all the timbers, but I thought we might get the eight or ten nearest the mud flats if we practiced till we had a system worked out.

At first we couldn't find a way to budge the heavy timbers. Our legs sank into the soft muck up to our thighs when we tried to drag one with ropes, and we were afraid we'd never be able to move them, even with the help of a flood tide. Each one of them was a foot and a half wide, a foot thick, and nearly thirty feet long. Worse still, there were old bent spikes and bolts sticking out of them that would snag in the eel grass and keep them from sliding.

It was Al Richardson who figured out a way that would work. We all lay on our backs behind the nearest timber, with our bottoms about a foot away from it and our knees doubled up. When I counted up to three we pushed out hard with our feet, and, even without a drop of water under it, the timber rolled over. All we had to do was to keep ooching up and rolling it, and in less than three minutes we had it out on the mud flat.

As soon as that timber was out on the mud, we scrambled up and floundered to the next one, flopped down, and started it rolling. By the time the tide began edging back through the eel grass we had nine timbers afloat.

With every inch the tide rose the timbers rolled easier. And when there was six or eight inches of water in the eel grass we didn't have to roll them. They were so nearly afloat that three boys, floundering along on their knees, could slide one into deep water. I hadn't planned to do any bossing, but somebody had to do it, and the boys didn't seem to mind my shouting and telling them what to do next. I split them into teams of threes, told each team which timber to take next, and what to do when one got snagged in the eel grass.

If you're just sitting on a bank, watching the tide come up or go down, it doesn't seem to rise or fall an inch an hour. But if you want it to stand still it seems to rise and fall like a pump handle. It didn't seem to me that we'd had more than five minutes when timbers would float before the flood was gone, and there was only a shimmer of water draining away between the blades of eel grass. Maybe it was just as well it went so quickly, because the boys, and even I who hadn't done much of the work, were tired and winded. As I looked around the marsh I could see only seven flags left, and they were all far back from the water, so I shouted to the boys and told them we had all we were going to take.

For the next hour we didn't do anything, except to tie our nineteen timbers together into four rafts, anchor them where the water was four or five feet deep, and lie on them while our backs and bellies sunburned. With the tide running out to sea, and with our wanting to get our rafts a mile upriver to Foster's Beach, there didn't seem much reason to do anything else for a while. The tide was too strong to paddle against, but if we waited for it to turn, about all we'd have to do would be to steer.

I think we might have wasted most of the day if the water hadn't been so cold, and if my conscience hadn't started bothering me. I'd told Mother we were going for paving blocks, but we hadn't picked up a single one, so I shouted, "I'll bet I know how we could make a lot more money today. There must be ten thousand paving blocks scattered around the marshes, and each one would make as much kindling as the bundles we sell at the store for six cents. It would be as easy to peddle as hot peanuts."

I wasn't a bit sure the boys would want to wade around in the mud any more, but it seemed to me that if I led the way they might follow. So I dived over the side and swam as fast as I could toward the mud bank. In Colorado I used to think I was a pretty good swimmer, but those Medford boys, brought up right beside the Mystic River, made me look like a mud turtle racing a school of trout.

It's funny how fast you can learn to do things by doing them. When we first came onto the marshes that morning we could hardly take a step without sinking up to our knees in the muck, but before we'd each picked up half a dozen armfuls of blocks there wasn't one of us who was sinking above his ankles. Without more than glancing, we could pick out the solidest tufts, and bounce from one to another—snatching up a block as we went—before we had time to break through. When the twelve o'clock whistle blew at the brickyards we had a pile of blocks at the edge of the mud bank that was nearly as big as a chicken coop. As soon as the whistle blew I shouted, "It's noon! Let's go eat our lunches."

"Why go over there?" somebody shouted back. "Why not let a couple bring our stuff over here while the rest of us go clamming?"

Scattered through the marshes there were pot holes, some of them as much as twelve or fifteen feet deep, and twenty feet or so wide. I think they were made by the tide dissolving and carrying out pockets of real fine clay, leaving the sides and bottoms firm and gravelly. The fattest clams to be found anywhere around Boston grew in the bottoms of the pot holes, and the Medford boys had a system for getting them out.

As soon as we'd drawn lots and the boys who lost had gone for our stuff the rest of us went clamming. I went with Al and Allie, but I wasn't very much help to them. Al led the way to a place where there were two big pot holes, right close to each other. He picked up a short, pointed stick that was lying near one of the holes, drew a deep breath and dived in. After a few seconds a gray cloud drifted up to the surface of the water, then a few bubbles, but I was scared to death that Al had drowned before he popped to the surface. And when he popped he came up as if he'd bounced off a springboard. His whole chest came above the water, then he rolled onto his back, ducked his head just enough to comb his hair, and swam to the bank. Before he was out of the water, Allie had picked up a stick and dived.

As soon as Al could catch his breath enough to talk, he told me, "It's your turn next. There's a big rock down there with a wire 'round it. Grab hold of the wire to keep yourself down, and plow up as much bottom as you can before you run out of breath. You'll have to dig deep if you want to get the fattest clams."

The only diving I'd ever done had been in the Platte River, and there weren't many places where it was more than knee-deep, so I'd never been under water for more than a couple of seconds at a time. Of course, I didn't tell that to Al, and as soon as Allie popped to the surface I grabbed a stick and dived in. But I didn't do any good. I wasn't more than three or four feet under water before I came to the top. "You can't make it in a dive alone," Al shouted at me. "You've got to swim to get down there."

I ducked my head and swam as hard as I could, but instead of going down I bumped into the bank. "Don't dog-paddle, you goop!" Al yelled at me when I had to come up for air. "Swim like a frog!"

I'd seen frogs swim plenty of times, so I pulled my knees up beside my ribs and kicked with my legs spread wide apart. Nothing happened, except that Al and Allie rolled around and laughed as if they'd gone crazy. After I'd tried a few more times, Al dived in and said, "Here, let me show you, you dumbbell!"

If I hadn't known I'd made a monkey of myself, I wouldn't have let Al call me a dumbbell, but I kept still and let him show me. He flipped over, so that his bottom stuck up like the tail of a feeding duck, then swept both arms back as he fluttered his feet. Within two seconds he was out of sight in the murky water.

I had to make five or six tries before I could get deep enough to grab hold of the wire on the rock, and by that time my lungs were so close to exploding that I had to come right up. But Al and Allie were experts. After they'd plowed up the bottom of the first hole, they let the clay settle while they plowed the second. Then they dived down with a leaky old bucket, and picked up the clams they'd dug loose.

I guess I slowed Al and Allie up more than I realized. We were the last ones back to the rafts, and we must have brought the fewest clams. There was nearly a bushel piled up in the middle of each raft, and the boys were opening them. Most of their jackknives were big toad-stabbers, and they didn't seem to mind how much they dulled the blades. A boy would pick up a clam, wiggle the blade of his knife into the crack between the shells, give it a little swing, and flip the top shell into the river. Another flip of the knife would turn the clam around in the bottom shell, and the boy would gulp it down as if it were a raw egg.

I wasn't much better at opening clams than I was at digging them. Every one I picked up was as stubborn as a mule. The first one kept his shells pinched so tight that it took me five minutes to wiggle my knife between them, and when I tried to pry the top shell off the blade snapped. "Not that way!" Al told me. "You've got to cut the muscle before you can flip the shell off."

I'd never known clams had muscles until Al opened one and showed me, and even after that I wasn't much good at opening them. But it was just as well. When I got one open I could hardly make myself swallow it.

Some of the boys made their whole lunch on clams, and then we rested and swam for about an hour before we went back to pick up more blocks. By quarter of four, when the tide turned, we had all four rafts stacked nearly three feet high with blocks, and only enough room at the front and back for a couple of boys. As soon as the tide began running upriver in good shape we gathered our boards, and one of the boys who could handle the hatchet real well cut them into paddles. With a boy kneeling at each corner, they edged the loaded rafts out into the current and paddled away up the river toward Foster's Beach.

Allie and I didn't go on the rafts, but put on our clothes and went to his house for the old running gear from his brother's wagon. The wheel hubs and turn plate had to be greased, and a couple of the tires that were loose had to be wedged tight. By the time we had it ready and pulled down to the beach the rafts were coming around the last bend in the river. We were barely undressed again before the first one turned in for a landing.

We were so anxious to see if my idea would work that we didn't wait for the last raft to get in before we tried it. We tossed part of the blocks off the first raft in, separated one timber from the others, and backed the running gear astraddle of it. As the wheels left the ground we pushed the axles along until the timber floated evenly, then chained the bolsters to it, leaving the front chain just loose enough that the wheels would turn. By the time we had half a dozen pull-ropes tied to the running gear the last raft was in, so I had part of the boys weight down the back end of the timber while the rest of us pulled on the ropes. When the wheels touched bottom the big timber hung evenly from the axles, and came up out of the water with a rush as we ran up the beach, howling like wild Indians.

Everything worked fine till we reached the upper edge of the beach, where it curved down steeply like the rim of a saucer. Then both ends of the timber dragged, and the front dug into the gravel like a plow. We were trying to drag it along when a voice from above us called, "For glory's sake, why don't you fetch it up slonchways? You'll never in this livin' world pull it up at all, at all, by main strength and awkwardness."

When we looked up Cop Watson was standing at the rim of the beach, twirling his night stick in a cartwheel and watching us. "Get it back in the water where 'twill float," he told us, "and drift it to that far corner, yonder where the eel grass commences. Then you can come up in a widenin' curve, and 'twill fetch you over the rim at the end o' the roadway."

Cop Watson not only told us how to get the timber up to the roadway, but he helped us. As soon as we'd pushed it back into the water and floated it into place, he came down and picked up the end of the wagon pole. He told us he was only going to do the steering for us, but he pulled harder than any four of us put together. It didn't take us a minute to get up onto the roadway.

We were all a little winded when we reached the roadway, and while we were resting Cop Watson said, "And now I've a notion I'll be havin' a fight to deal with when you go to divvyin' it up."

"No, sir," I told him. "We had our deal all made before we started: I get half for having the idea, and everybody else gets share and share alike."

"A half?" he said, and looked at me out of one corner of his eye.

"Yes, sir," I said. "But it was my idea, and none of us would have got any if I hadn't thought of it, and one of these timbers must be worth. . . ."

I stopped because I could see that Cop Watson wasn't listening to me. He stood for a minute, looking at the ground and rubbing his mustache across his cheeks with the back of a hand. Then he looked up, nodded his head, and said, " 'Tis fair enough; fair enough, lads. 'Tis ever the man what gets the idea and sets it to goin' that gets the gravy, not them what works with their hands. Now you take old John D. Like as not he never done a day's work with his hands in all the livin' world. And look where he's at now. How many o' them timbers did you salvage?"

"Nineteen," I told him.

He pointed his finger at each one of us as he counted, and asked, "Would you be tellin' me how you're goin' to divvy nineteen into half, and a half into sixteens?"

"Well," I told him, "we got enough paving blocks to make a pile bigger than all the timbers put together. Some of the boys might want to take blocks instead of a timber; the blocks won't have to be sawed to make fire wood, and the timbers will."

"True. True," he said. "And how many blocks do you call the equal of a beam?"

"We haven't thought about that yet," I told him. "How many would you think was fair?"

Cop Watson went over to the pile of blocks we'd tossed up over the rim, bounced one of them in his hand a few times, and said, "Well now, there's two ways o' lookin' at it: the work, and

what comes out of it. Them that takes block'll have no sawin'
to do, and that's half o' the job, so them that takes beams ought
to get the double out of it when it's in shape for burnin'." He ran
a little finger inside the circle of his ear, and looked back and
forth between the block in his hand and the big timber hanging
from the axles of the running gear. "How about callin' it a hunderd even?" he asked. "How many of yous would take a hunderd
blocks in the place of a timber?"

The boys divided exactly even. The laziest eight said they'd
take blocks, and the other eight said nothing.

With the division all worked out, we decided that we'd take
one load to our house and then a load to some other boy's house,
alternately, and they'd draw straws to find out in what order
we'd take them: the longest straw first and the shortest last.
That was the fairest way we could do it, because we had no
idea of how many we could haul that afternoon. Nobody could
work on Sunday, and any that didn't get hauled before Monday were pretty apt to be swiped. It was Cop Watson who
figured out the scheme that made it possible for us to haul every
last block and timber before the nine o'clock curfew sounded.

Once a timber was up on the roadway there was no sense
in seventeen of us going to deliver it; four or five could trot and
pull the load. So I picked the biggest four, and told the others
to watch that our rafts didn't drift away as the tide rose, and
that they might lug all the blocks up to the roadway, where
they'd be handy for loading.

We took the first timber to our house, wheeling it to one edge
of the back lawn, and it unloaded as easily as it had loaded. All
I had to do was to put down blocks and have the boys pry up
one end at a time, while I pulled the bolt and drew the chain
out from under.

I don't believe we were gone from the beach more than fifteen
minutes, and when we got back Cop Watson was showing the
boys how to make a wagon body with some pieces of driftwood
board, some bent nails, and the hatchet. "There's no sense at
all, at all, in squanderin' daylight," he told me as we came trot-

ting up with the empty running gear. "Them dry blocks don't weigh next to nothin', and with a body on that contraption you can be haulin' a load o' blocks atop and a beam beneath."

Once we knew how to get the beams from the river to the roadway it wasn't a very tough job. It didn't take over five minutes to hook on and snake one up, and with the driftwood box to hold them, seventeen of us could toss on a hundred blocks in almost nothing flat. Whoever was going to get the timber or the blocks went along to show us where to unload, and by making two deliveries at one trip we saved nearly half our time.

When we delivered the third load at our house, half the kids in the neighborhood were there to watch us, and Mother came out to tell us what a fine job we'd done. When I told her we'd just started and that we still had eight more timbers to bring home, she said, "Gracious sakes! You boys must be bone-tired and nearly starved to death. After one or two more loads you must stop for supper and some rest."

"We can't," I told her. "If we do we'll never be finished by curfew time, and anything we don't haul tonight will probably be swiped by Monday."

"Oh, you mustn't work right through without eating," she told me, but she didn't say right out and out that I'd have to stop for supper, so I just told her we'd be back in a little while, and we trotted away.

Our next deliveries were nearly down to Salem Street, so it was almost six o'clock before we got back to our house with a load. I didn't want to give Mother too much of a chance to come out and tell me I'd have to stop for supper, so we just dropped the timber, tipped the body up to spill the blocks, and started back out of the yard. We'd only gone as far as the kitchen steps when Grace opened the door and said, "Don't be in such a rush! You wait right where you are till I get down there!"

Grace didn't often try to boss me around when I was with other boys, and I think I might have told her to mind her own business, but she closed the door too soon, so all I could do was wait. But we didn't have to wait long. In another minute she opened the door and came down the steps with the bean pot in her hands. It must have been straight out of the oven, because she was carrying it with pot-holder mittens. Mother was right behind her with a big pan of gingerbread, wrapped in a towel, and a box of plates and cups and knives and forks. "Now just hold on a minute," she told me as she set them on the block box. "Gracie will be right here with a loaf of brown-bread and a pail of cocoa. She's going along to see that you boys get some supper into you. You can eat it right down there at the river, and she'll bring the dishes home when you're through. Now do be careful, and don't strain yourselves with those great pieces of lumber."

I think the sliding at the clay pit must have done something to Grace. She didn't try to be a bit grown-up that evening, but rode down to the beach on the old wagon, and laughed and joked with the boys all the time she was dishing up our supper. Half a dozen of the boys told me I didn't know how lucky I was to have a sister like her, and, of course, I didn't mention the way she usually tried to boss me around. As soon as we'd eaten they made me take the next load right back to our house, and I think it was mainly so the bigger boys could go along and ride Grace back on the wagon.

With every trip we made the tide rose higher and the pull up the beach was easier. After supper nobody doubted that we'd get the job finished before curfew time, so we didn't bother with turns any longer, but went wherever we could deliver a timber and a load of blocks right in the same neighborhood. It was half-past eight when we pulled away from Foster's Beach with the last timber and the last paving block. That was the eleventh timber we took to our house, and we must have taken more than a thousand blocks along with them. After it was un-loaded I helped Allie pull the running gear back to its place be-hind Dion's barn, and I was running up our back steps just as the curfew bell rang.

23

Every Little Bit Helps

W E'D had to hurry so much in bringing the wood home Saturday night that we didn't have time to be very neat about it. We just pulled the running gear onto any part of our back lawn where there was room for the wheels, dropped the timber and dumped off the load of paving blocks. When I took Mother out to see it in daylight Sunday morning she said, "My! My! Did you ever see anything like it in your life! Why, those big sticks will keep us in firewood for a couple of years, and I don't know how we'll ever use up all the kindling those paving blocks will make. I don't see how in the world you boys managed to do it."

"It wasn't hard," I told her. "No matter how big a piece of wood is, it doesn't weigh anything when it's in water, and the wagon wheels made it easy to bring them home. I didn't plan that we'd use all the blocks ourselves. If Philip and I split them into kindling I'll bet we'd find lots of people who would be glad to buy it for twenty-five cents a cart load. That's a good bargain, because they'd have to pay twice that much for kindling at the store."

"Why, that's a splendid idea," Mother said. "In that way you and Philip would have a little business of your own, and you

could put your profits away toward buying the school clothing you children will need next fall. But, good heavens! From
the way you're growing you'll need some new clothes before
summer gets here. Are you sure you're not making a pig of
yourself at the store, Son?"

"No, ma'am, I'm not," I told her. "I never eat more than two
pieces of candy in any one day, and I only eat cheese and
crackers when Mr. Haushalter gives them to me."

"Mmmmm, hmmmm, but right now we'll have to think some
about clearing up this yard," Mother said. "I wouldn't be able
to hang out laundry with these big sticks scattered all around
the way they are, and what's more they'll soon kill all the grass
that's under them. Do you think they could be piled up neatly,
over there in one corner?"

"Well," I told her, "if I can get all the boys over here we
could lie on our backs and roll them over that way, but we
could never pile them up; it would take a derrick to lift one.
But if we had a good two-handled saw, Philip and I could cut
them into pieces right where they are. Then they wouldn't be
too heavy to pile up."

"Hmmmm, together with your job at the store that would
take the rest of the summer," Mother said, "and long before that
our lawn would be completely ruined. I wonder if Uncle Frank
could give you any help with them."

I'd been so busy for the past few days that I hadn't even
thought about Uncle Frank. But when Mother mentioned his
name I wanted to show him the job I'd done more than I wanted
anything else in the world. Of course, I knew he couldn't lift
one of those timbers any more than I could. And even if he
were strong enough, he couldn't do it on Sunday, but I said,
"I'll run right over and get him now."

"No, no," Mother said quickly, "not now. Maybe after church,
and after we've had our dinner, you might go over and talk to
him about it. I'm not at all sure he'll be able to help us, but we
must find some way of moving them, for I simply must have this

space for hanging out laundry, and we can't ruin Mr. Perkins' nice lawn."

All through Sunday School and church I tried to figure out some way of moving those timbers and piling them up, and as soon as we'd finished dinner I ran over to Uncle Frank's house. I knew that if I tried to tell him anything about the wood it might sound like bragging, so I just told him we needed some help at our house as soon as he could come over.

"Shall I bring my tools?" he asked. "You know, I won't be able to do any work outside on Sunday, don't you?"

"Yes, sir," I said, "I know it. But this isn't a job anybody could do with tools. It's one Philip and I can't do by ourselves, and Mother wondered if you could help us with it."

"Don't you think you'd better tell me what the job is, so I'll know what I might need?" Uncle Frank asked.

"Well, you'd need a derrick more than anything else," I told him, "but I can't explain the job to you. I could show you better when we get over there. Do you think you'd be able to come now?"

All the way over to our house I kept talking about something else, so Uncle Frank wouldn't have a chance to ask me any more questions. Then, when we turned down the driveway at the side of the fire station and he saw our back yard, he shouted, "For the love of Pete! Did a tidal wave strike you?"

"No, sir," I told him, "but a flood tide struck the river, and I guess you know the Wellington Bridge caught fire and the firemen tore out two big sections of it. Well, this is just some of the pieces I picked up and brought home."

"You what?" he said, as if he'd caught me lying to him.

"Well, I didn't pick them up all alone," I told him. "Some of the other boys helped me, and I helped them, and we divided fifty-fifty. This was my share. But what I need to know is how to pile the big timbers up. Mother says we'll have to put them in a nice neat pile, over there in the corner, but Philip and I couldn't budge one of them."

"How in the name of Moses did you ever get them home?" he asked.

"That was easy enough," I told him. "We just chained wagon wheels on top of them while they were floating in the water at Foster's Beach. There was nothing to wheeling them home."

"Anybody might know you were Charlie Moody's boy," he said, "and it looks to me as if you folks were going to get along all right . . . if enough bridges burn down. But that isn't getting these joists piled, is it, and I'll be jiggered if I can tell you how to do it without sawing them up. Ten men couldn't lift one of them."

On warm Sunday afternoons the firemen sometimes used to bring their chairs out and sit in the sun to read the paper. The lieutenant and the other regular fireman at our station came out while Uncle Frank and I were talking about the timbers. The lieutenant stood his chair down, then came over and said to Uncle Frank, "Wasn't that quite a job those kids did yesterday? Bill and I were standing by to give 'em a hand with the unloading, but they didn't seem to need it."

"Don't know yet how they ever did it," Uncle Frank told him, "but they'll sure need plenty of help to get them moved from where they dropped them. He says he wants to pile them up over in that corner."

"What you going to do with 'em after you get 'em piled up?" the lieutenant asked me.

"Saw them up for firewood if I can get hold of a two-handled saw," I told him.

"Ought to make good kindling," he said. "A man couldn't find better, but this pitchy stuff would burn awful fast for firewood. A cord wouldn't go as far as half a ton of coal." Then he asked Uncle Frank, "How do you figure on moving and stacking 'em?"

"Don't know," Uncle Frank told him. "Soft as this ground is, a man couldn't move them on rollers. And what's more, he couldn't pry them up to get rollers underneath without tearing the lawn to pieces."

"Have to lay planks down and skid 'em," the lieutenant said. "Might be Bill and I'll have a chance to give it a try tomorrow. That is, if we don't get called out. Little late now for overheated stoves, and too early for brush fires; we might get a chance at it. Got an extra horse here we're training right now; wouldn't hurt him to get a little exercise."

Both Uncle Frank and I thanked the lieutenant and he started away toward his chair. He'd gone only halfway when he turned back to Uncle Frank and said, "Hear you're quite a cribbage player. Drop in some evening when you've nothing better to do."

After Uncle Frank had told the lieutenant that he'd come to the firehouse some night to play cribbage, and after he'd talked to Mother for a little while, I walked back to his house with him. "I wish we'd brought along the big cross-cut saw we had for sawing railroad ties in Colorado," I told him as soon as we were started. "With a saw like that Philip and I could whack those timbers into stove lengths pretty fast, but I don't think a buck-saw would work on stuff that big, and two-handled cross-cuts cost a lot of money."

"No need of buying one," Uncle Frank told me. "Father's got a good five-footer down to the farm, and he won't be using it this time of year. I'll be going to see him on my next trip into Brunswick, and I'll bring it back for you. You'll probably raise hobb with it on those old spikes, but if you don't yank it, so's to break a tooth, I can keep it tuned up for you. I'll have it up here by Wednesday."

After I came home from Uncle Frank's I told Philip about our going into partnerships on the kindling wood business, and about our going to save the profits to buy school clothes for everybody that fall. He couldn't have been more tickled if I'd told him he was going to be President of the United States. The first thing he did was to run over to Uncle Frank's to borrow his hatchet, and Mother had to scold him for going out to split kindling on Sunday.

Philip had never really been lazy, but he'd never been much of a hand to hurry either, and he didn't like to get up quite as early in the mornings as I did. But going in partnership worked like sulphur and molasses on him. Monday morning he woke me up and wanted us to go splitting kindling when it was still dark in the corners of our room. Then he was the first one to be excused from the breakfast table, and he was splitting as fast as he could go when I left for my job at the store. At noon Mother had to tell him he couldn't split any more until after he'd picked up the laundry baskets, or until every block was off the lawn and stacked at the end of the garden.

When I came home from work that evening it would have

been hard to see that our back lawn had ever been messed
up—except for a few little dents and scraped places. The big
timbers were stacked up in the corner by the firehouse driveway; two-wide and five-high, with the odd one lying on top like
a ridgepole. Philip was splitting kindling, and Muriel and Hal
were stacking up the last few paving blocks.

"You oughta been here! You oughta been here, Ralph!" Hal
called as he ran to meet me. "The firemens and their horse piled
up all the big sticks, and Muriel and I piled up all the little
ones. You oughta see that horse pull! I'll betcha he can pull
more than an elephant! Look at the holes his feet made in the
driveway when he slided 'em up the boards to the top of the
pile! Philip says he's going to have this kindling all chopped
up by tomorrow night, and he's going to sell it for at least a
hundred dollars. I'll bet we'll be rich when he gets it all sold."

The first thing I did was to go over to the firehouse, to thank
the lieutenant for piling up our timbers, and to tell him we'd be
glad to bring over as much kindling as they needed. And I just
happened to mention that Uncle Frank had taught me how to
play cribbage when we were staying at his house. He told me
that I didn't need to thank them, that it was good exercise for
both them and the horse, and that the City of Medford furnished them with all the kindling they could use. Then, just
before I left, he told me to come over some evening and we'd
have a rousing good game of cribbage.

My partnership with Philip was about as lopsided as my
partnership with the other boys. I might have had the idea,
but he did most of the work—he and Muriel and Hal. Of
course, I helped with the splitting, because Mother made Philip
quit and go to bed at eight o'clock, and she let me work from
supper time till curfew. But Muriel went from house to house,
taking orders, and Philip and Hal made all the deliveries. With
light kindling Hal could be as much help about loading the
cart and carrying armfuls into the houses as if he'd been four
or five years older.

Right at the beginning we'd decided to heap every cart

load in good shape, so we'd be giving people a real bargain, and I think our first customers must have told others about it. Muriel didn't have to go more than two blocks from home before she'd sold all the kindling the blocks would make, and some of the ladies took as many as four loads.

Even Grace had a part in our partnership. Every time Philip came home with a quarter he gave it to her, and every night at supper time she told us how much our profits had been. The profits were almost as much as the sales, because our only expense was for a hatchet of our own.

Uncle Frank brought us Grandfather's long saw on Wednesday evening, but we didn't have any time to use it during the next week. Muriel was so far ahead of us on kindling orders that it kept us jumping to split blocks, and they lasted till almost curfew time on Tuesday. When Grace made her report on Wednesday, every last stick of kindling had been delivered, and she said we had $21.68 in our treasury. Of course, it wasn't a real treasury; just Mother's Wedgwood sugar bowl. At first Mother wouldn't believe the amount was right, but after dinner Grace brought the sugar bowl and counted the money out in three-dollar piles on the table. It came out just the way Grace said it would; anything to do with figures or money usually did.

"My! My!" Mother said as she counted the piles, "I can hardly believe that you little children have made so much money in so short a time. Why, that will give us money for new shoes all around, and new suits for you boys, and . . ."

"And that isn't all," I told her. "With kindling wood selling the way it is we wouldn't be very smart to burn up the big timbers for firewood. A cord of that pitchy stuff wouldn't go any further than half a ton of coal, and half a ton of coal only costs three dollars and a cord of wood would make . . . let's see . . . there's about a square foot and a half of wood to a load of kindling, and . . ."

"And a cord is four feet, by four feet, by eight feet," Grace broke in, "and that's a hundred and twenty-eight cubic feet, divided by one and a half is eighty-three loads of kindling, times a quarter is twenty dollars and seventy-five cents a cord. And if each of those timbers is a foot by a foot and a half, and thirty feet long; that's forty-five times eleven, divided by one twenty-eight is about four cords, so that would amount to eighty-three dollars, and two tons of coal would cost twelve dollars, leaving a profit of seventy-one dollars."

Grace had me mixed up before she got through the four times four times eight, and I think she'd lost Mother sooner than that, but we both knew Grace well enough to know she'd be right. "*My My!*" Mother almost shouted. "Why, that's nearly a hundred dollars altogether! Well! I guess we won't have to worry much about you children being well-dressed for school next autumn." She sat for a minute, pinching her lips together with her thumb and finger, then looked up at me and said, "Ralph, I'm going to let you and Philip stay out of school tomorrow afternoon and go to Boston for new shoes. You both need them badly, and I think you need a little holiday before you tackle the rest of that job."

24

A May Basket for Mary Emma

I T SEEMS as if good luck always comes in showers, and we were right where half a dozen of those showers fell during the month of April. The last Sunday morning of that month we had the biggest turnout at our church that we'd had any Sunday except Easter. By the time Sunday School was over the church was already more than half filled, and people were coming in by sixes and sevens, but Mother and Elizabeth weren't among them.

We waited out in front of the church while more and more people went in, then we walked up Otis Street to meet Mother and hurry her along. When we got back there were a dozen or so people standing in the vestibule, and the ushers were splitting them up in ones and twos to find seats for them. As Mother whispered to the younger children, telling them to sit real still and not disturb the people they'd be seated with, an usher put his hand under her elbow and said, "Right this way, Mrs. Moody."

She had just turned back to us and whispered, "You will be very careful, won't you, children?" when the usher motioned with his fingers for all of us to come along. He led us out through the crowd in the vestibule, and clear up to the third row from the front; the one where we'd sat ever since we'd moved to Medford. I don't think there were six other seats left in the whole church, but our six were empty. While we were going into the pew at least a dozen people turned to nod their heads and smile at Mother. Sometimes the things that made her the happiest were the ones that made her come the nearest to crying. Before she could find the right number for the opening hymn she had to lift her veil up and wipe the tears out of her eyes.

The sermon was a good one, but long, and with such a crowd in the church it took us nearly fifteen minutes to get out. I don't know how so many people knew us, with our having gone to that church only four months, but a lot of them did. We could move only a step or two at a time, because so many people were coming out of the pews, and it seemed as if half of them turned to tell Mother what well-behaved children she had. I could only walk along with my head down, because I was sure that, sooner or later, they'd find out about my name being on the bad-boy book.

It was a beautiful spring day, and the people didn't seem to be in any hurry to get away from the church. When we came down the steps they were standing around in little groups on the lawn, and up and down the sidewalk, visiting and talking. It looked to me as if Mother's customers were having a little convention under the big maple tree on the lawn. Every one of them were there, with their husbands and a dozen or so other men and women I didn't know. We were nearly out to the sidewalk when Mrs. Humphrey came toward us and said, "Oh, Mrs. Moody, I'm so glad to see you this morning. Won't you bring your lovely children over for a minute? I'd like my husband and my friends to meet them."

Of course, Mrs. Humphrey knew Philip and Muriel and me, because we'd delivered her laundry. After she'd introduced Mother and us, she said, "And now, Mrs. Moody, I'm going to let you introduce the others, for I'm ashamed to say I don't know their names."

Hal and Elizabeth didn't get introduced at all, because Mother started with Grace. "This is Gracie, my right hand," she said. "It is she who does all the gentlemen's shirts and collars, and helps me with the fancier garments."

Mr. Humphrey tipped his hat to Grace and said, "You're an artist. I've never before had my shirts so beautifully done."

"They're both artists," Mrs. Humphrey told the other people. She ran her fingers up through the folds of the jabot she was wearing, and said, "Everything they touch comes back like a work of art, and I have yet to receive one piece crushed in delivery. Her children are just as painstaking as she is."

There were quite a few other nice things said, then several of the ladies I didn't know asked Mother if she'd be able to do their laundry. "Oh my!" she told them, "I don't know if we could handle so many; our lines are pretty full now on our busiest days."

"It's largely my fault," Mrs. Humphrey told them. "I've been selfish in sending Mrs. Moody all my flat work." Then she turned to Mother and asked, "If I were to make different arrangements for it would you be able to handle the others?"

Grace was standing with one foot right close to mine, and it bumped me a little tap before Mother had a chance to say, "Oh, I'd hate to inconvenience you that much, Mrs. Humphrey, but we would be able to handle more of the fancier garments." Before we left both Mrs. Humphrey and Mrs. Nickerson said they'd make other arrangements for their flat work, and Mother had said she'd try to handle all the new customers if she could have until Saturdays to get their work finished.

I carried Elizabeth and we all walked quietly until we'd reached the end of Otis Street. But when we'd turned the corner onto Washington, out of sight of the people coming from church, Mother threw an arm around Grace's waist, and they took two or three skipping steps. When they stopped, Grace slapped her hands together and said, "Well, I guess we're over the hill."

"I'm sure of it," Mother told her. "Let's hurry right home and fix a special treat for dinner."

During the last couple of days of April, most of the talking around Franklin School was about May baskets. If a boy liked some particular girl and wanted her to be his girl he didn't very often tell her so. He waited for May Day and then hung a May basket on her door just after dark, then he ran. You didn't ever put your name on the basket, but wrote the girl's name on a little card you tucked inside. Then she was supposed to guess who it was from by the handwriting.

I hadn't thought much about liking one girl any better than the others, or about hanging a May basket, until the boys at school began talking about it so much. And then I began thinking about Evelyn Gorham a good deal. Evelyn sat right back of me at school, and she was the prettiest girl in our class: small and dark, with brown eyes and coal-black hair.

Of course, I didn't know how to make a pretty May basket, and I wanted to have a real nice one for Evelyn, so at daylight on May Day morning I rapped on the girls' bedroom door. When Grace opened it a crack and asked me what I wanted I told her I had to talk to her for a minute out in the hall. Sometimes Grace could be a bit grumpy when she was waked up too early, but that morning she was as nice as pie. After I'd told her about Evelyn, and wanting to hang a May basket for her, and not knowing how to make one, she said, "That's easy. I could make you a real pretty one if I had some colored crepe paper, but that would cost about a dime, and if you want a really nice one you'd have to spend a quarter for candy and nuts to fill it. Why don't you take thirty-five cents out of the kindling treasury?"

"That's partnership money," I told her, "and it wouldn't be fair to Philip."

"Oh, piffle!" she said. "Philip wouldn't care." Then she sort of giggled, and asked me, "How do you know he hasn't got a girl, too? Maybe he'd like to hang a May basket, and I could make two as easy as one. Let's go wake him up and ask him."

Philip's eyes sparkled when Grace told him about the basket she was going to make for me and asked him if he wanted to hang one. "Sure I do," he told her, "but I'm not going to waste it on any girl; I'm going to hang it for Mother."

Grace tried to tell him that you only hung a May basket to a girl you wanted for your sweetheart, but that didn't make any difference to Philip; he wouldn't change his mind. At noon he met me at Uebel's drug store, and we picked out the crepe paper and nuts and candy. In the afternoon Grace made us two beautiful baskets, but she did it up in her room where Mother couldn't see them.

As soon as we'd eaten supper that night I changed into my Sunday clothes, and twilight was just turning into darkness when I hung my basket on Evelyn's doorknob and rang the bell. Then I ran back toward Washington Street, but I didn't run awfully fast, and I was careful to slow up as I went under the street lamp. I wasn't too sure that Evelyn would know my handwriting.

I hadn't been home more than five minutes, and we were all in the kitchen when our own doorbell rang. Grace and I looked around quickly to be sure Philip was there, because we hadn't planned for him to hang his basket until Mother had gone into the parlor for the evening. Philip looked as puzzled as we were. It was about a minute before Grace said, "Mother, that was our doorbell."

"Yes, Daughter," Mother said, "you run along and answer it; it must be a May basket."

"Hmmmmff!" Grace sniffed. "Nobody'd be hanging me a May basket, and Muriel and Elizabeth are too little. It's probably one of our new customers to see you."

"Well, you run right along," Mother told her. "I'll bet a cookie it's a May basket."

Grace made another little sniffing sound, but she went to the door. And when she came back she was carrying a May basket nearly as big as a shoe box. At first she tried to act as if she weren't a bit excited, but her eyes were as bright as blue-

bells when she passed her basket around for all of us to have a piece of candy.

Philip could hardly wait for a chance to hang his May basket for Mother. Ever since supper he'd had it hidden under the back steps, but there wasn't any chance for him to sneak out and hang it for another half-hour. Twice more before that half-hour was up our doorbell had rung again, and both times it was a May basket for Grace. We were all sitting in the parlor when it rang the second time, and Grace ran to the door as fast as she could go, but when she came back she wouldn't tell us if she'd seen the boy. I think she had all right, and that it was one of the older boys who had been sliding at the clay pit with us, way back in the winter, but Grace wouldn't admit it.

Mother seemed as happy about Grace's getting the baskets as Grace was herself. Her eyes sparkled just as much, and she was telling us about her very first May basket when Philip said he was going to the kitchen for a drink of water. He wasn't gone more than a minute before our bell rang again, and that time we all made Mother go to answer the door. Before she had time to get back Philip had run around to the kitchen door and come in. He was bouncing up and down in his chair when Mother came back to the parlor with a big smile on her face. She held the pretty basket out toward Grace and said, "Another basket for you, Gracie. My, you must be the most popular girl in town!"

"Oh, no!" Grace said. "No boy would ever hang a basket as fancy as that one to anybody but his very best girl, and I'm nobody's very best girl. Look and see what it says on the card."

Mother looked a little puzzled for a second, but I think she guessed from the looks on our faces that we knew something about the basket. She sat down on the edge of her chair, set the basket on her knees, and took the card out. She had only glanced at it when she jumped up, dropping basket, card, and all. She was half laughing and half crying as she ran across to Philip's chair, dropped down on her knees, and hugged him

up tight to her. While she was loving him I picked up the card
she'd dropped. Philip had printed on it:

To M A R Y   E M M A
F R OM   H ER   B E ST   L OV E R

As soon as Mother could talk, she brushed the tears away
from her eyes and said, "Oh, children, hasn't the Lord been
good to us! Just think of it! At the first of January we left
Colorado, not knowing where we'd find a place to lay our heads,
or if we'd ever again have good friends and a home we could
call our own. And here it is only May." Then she hugged Philip
to her again.

About the Author

RALPH OWEN MOODY was born December 16, 1898, in Rochester, N. H. His father was a farmer whose illness forced the family to move to Colorado when Ralph was eight years old. The family's life in the new surroundings is told from the point of view of the boy himself in *Little Britches* (1950). The farm failed and the family moved into Littleton, Colorado, when Ralph was about eleven. Soon after, the elder Moody died of pneumonia, leaving Ralph as the oldest boy, the man of the family. After a year or so—described in *Man of the Family* (1951) and *The Home Ranch* (1956)—Mrs. Moody brought her three sons and three daughters back to Medford, Mass., where Ralph completed his formal education through the eighth grade of grammar school. This is the period of *Mary Emma & Company* (1961). Later, Ralph joined his maternal grandfather on his farm in Maine—the period covered in *The Fields of Home* (1953).

In spite of his farming experience, Ralph Moody was not destined to be a farmer. He abandoned the land because his wife was determined to raise her family (they have three children) in the city. He completed his high-school studies in the evening and continued his education in university extension classes.

"When I was twenty-one," he writes, "I got a diary as a birthday present and I wrote in it that I was going to work as hard as I could, save fifty thousand dollars by the time I was fifty, and then start writing." True to his word, he did start writing on the night of his fiftieth birthday.

—Adapted from the *Wilson Library Bulletin*